Behaviour in the Early Years

Behaviour in the Early Years

Second Edition

Angela Glenn,
Jacquie Cousins and
Alicia Helps

Routledge
Taylor & Francis Group

LONDON AND NEW YORK

First edition published 2004 by David Fulton Publishers

This second edition published 2011
by Routledge
2 Park Square, Milton Park, Abingdon, Oxon, OX14 4RN

Simultaneously published in the USA and Canada
by Routledge
270 Madison Avenue, New York, NY 10016

Routledge is an imprint of the Taylor & Francis Group, an informa business

© 2011 Angela Glenn, Jacquie Cousins and Alicia Helps

Typeset in Times New Roman by Saxon Graphics Ltd, Derby
Printed and bound in Great Britain by
The MPG Books Group

British Library Cataloguing in Publication Data
A catalogue record for this book is available from the British Library

Library of Congress Cataloging-in-Publication Data
Glenn, Angela.
  Behaviour in the early years / by Angela Glenn, Jacquie Cousins and Alicia Helps. — 2nd ed.
    p. cm.
  Rev. ed. of : Managing extreme behaviour in the early years, c2009.
  1. Problem children—Education (Preschool)—England—Medway. 2. Education, Preschool—England—Medway. I. Helps, Alicia. II. Cousins, Jacquie. III. Glenn, Angela, Managing extreme behaviour in the early years. IV. Title.
  LC4803.G72M433 2011
  649'.153—dc22
                                                        2010025141

ISBN13: 978-0-415-58435-7 (pbk)
ISBN13: 978-0-203-83506-7 (ebk)

CONTENTS

INTRODUCTION

This book was written in response to requests for advice received from all sorts of people working with young children in a range of early years settings. Experience in delivering in-service training sessions and professional development courses has shown us that colleagues are looking for straightforward guidance in dealing with the challenges presented by many of the children they meet – particularly in matters concerning behaviour.

We have put together a range of common situations and suggested some 'tried and tested' approaches. There is no magic wand and these simple approaches will not always work. There will be children whose needs are more complex and who therefore need more expert intervention.

However, the majority of children will respond to consistent, 'firm but fair' handling with lots of praise and positive reinforcement.

As will be seen from the examples given, it can sometimes be very difficult to be clear about the causes of children's difficulties, but we do know that the child is trying to tell us something through his behaviour. He does not have the verbal skills of an adult and therefore we need to be sensitive to what it is that the child is attempting to communicate. This is easier said than done when the child is behaving very badly, but we hope this easily accessible book will be one way of helping you to understand

what the child is trying to tell you as well as providing practical ideas to deal with difficult situations. Sections 1, 2 and 3 of the book deal with some ideas and strategies that can be easily absorbed into the daily routine. Basically, good practice for children with special educational needs is good practice for all children.

It can be difficult to provide with any accuracy a 'diagnosis' for a child at the pre-school stage. We can't always differentiate between the child who has neurological difficulties such as autistic spectrum disorder (ASD) and the child who has symptoms of anxiety caused by emotional stress. Both children may develop repetitive and immature behaviour that makes them feel more secure, and both could present as being withdrawn and not responding to instructions.

When a referral to a specialist professional is made, however, it will be very useful if the practitioner concerned can offer accurate observations and details of the strategies that have/have not been successful. The pre-school setting can provide very useful information in advising the professional about social, cognitive and emotional aspects of the child's functioning. The checklists and recording forms provided in Appendix 1 will enable practitioners to keep track of what they see and what they do in an easy, accessible format.

(We have used the convention of referring to the child as 'him' and the practitioner as 'her' purely in order to avoid clumsiness in the text. This is not to suggest that children with behaviour difficulties are always boys, or that staff are always women.)

This second edition of our book will cover the following additional areas:

- a new addition entitled 'From Birth to Toddler' that includes some ideas about how to manage those developmental stages;
- additional case studies including those around birth to toddler, some specialized case studies regarding children who may be on the autistic spectrum and demonstrate a wide range of behaviours, some case studies with regard to safeguarding issues;
- an addition to the section about managing staff that will cover some brief ideas about the role of the teaching assistant;
- and finally, an additional Section 5 entitled 'Safeguarding' that covers important issues regarding child protection.

Ten tips for good behaviour management

- Adopt a simple and easy-to-follow behaviour policy and share it with all the staff, helpers and parents.

- Keep lines of communication open with all concerned.

- Involve parents/carers right from the beginning: be sensitive and offer support rather than recrimination.

- Be factual when talking to parents/carers – opinions leave you open to having to justify yourself.

- Keep a list of observations about the child's behaviour, i.e. what actually happens.

- Remember to develop the child's strengths as well as tackling problems.

- Focus on one particular behaviour at a time: behaviour difficulties can be very complex, but a small change in how you respond to a child can result in success on which you can build.

- Concentrate on what is actually happening in your setting and what you have some control over. It is important to understand as much as possible about the child's home life, but you have to accept that it may prove difficult to influence.

- Be consistent.

- Remember, there are no magic answers – what works for one child may not work for another.

SECTION 1

From birth to toddler

Step 1: Be consistent

Step 2: Use praise and rewards

Step 3: Provide good models

Step 4: Guide the child

Step 5: Ignore bad behaviour

Step 6: Remove from the scene

Step 7: Apply sanctions

Some additional ideas

The birth of a newborn baby is usually a very joyous event and that baby is usually born into a family that includes many relations and also a network of friends each with their own ideas on child rearing.

The first few months will be a time of adapting to a new family member who will very soon establish a personality of his own. Most babies go through a separation anxiety stage at about nine months where they may become very anxious when away from the main carer(s). Babies have emotions and needs from birth and initially express them through crying, but gradually babies gain increasing mobility by initially crawling or rolling and can go and reach out for things and go to things themselves. At this stage the main aim is to think mainly about hygiene and safety for your baby.

Gradually as your baby becomes more mobile they become more independent and are more exploratory. This exploration can lead to problems and is the essential stage where parents or carers need to be very cautious and make clear to the child what they can and what they can't do. A firm, low voice usually works well. Although some of the antics seem funny, it is important not to laugh, as the child will think this is a game and will carry on with the game as long as possible. This would eventually result in the adult becoming very frustrated and very annoyed, sending a very mixed message to the child. Gradually as the child becomes more aware of his environment, the type of behaviour can continue when the child knows it can get a response. It can be at this early stage that parents can begin to feel demoralized so that they are unable to manage their child.

This is also the stage when children want to do more but need more adult help and demand it more if they don't get the support needed. From about 18 months as the child's mobility increases, he becomes a toddler and forms stronger ideas about likes and dislikes and acquires a will of his own, often a very strong will.

This is the stage of the 'Terrible Twos' as it is often called. When the toddler wants something, he wants it when *he* wants it and he feels others are preventing him from getting this. At this stage the child will not have developed sufficient self-control, nor will he be interested in bargains or threats.

Parents can imagine that a child who is able to speak is also able to understand. This is where difficulties arise, as parents may try to reason with a child who has not sufficiently developed emotionally to deal with the frustrations he is feeling. This is certainly a challenging time for parents and carers, as stroppiness and inability to reason often leads to tantrums.

Remember the 3 C's – be clear, concise and calm:

- Be clear in what you say and focus on one aspect at a time.
- Be very concise and use as few words as possible so as not to confuse the child.
- Say everything very calmly and keep repeating things calmly.

What works with toddlers?

- Set very clear boundaries.

- Keep as regular a routine as possible.

- Adults working with children should ensure that they are all using the same approach, as children quickly learn how to manipulate adults.

- Ensure the child is clear that the adults are in control and will not give in to any tantrum pressure, however persevering the child is.

- Some children enjoy a picture representation of what is happening that day. A strip of paper could be placed in a specific place with pictures or photographs of what is happening that day. This can be backed with Velcro® or Blu-tack®. It can be for the whole day or for specific parts of the day such as bedtime. This particular strip of card could show having a bath, getting pyjamas on, story at bedtime, lights out. Sometimes photographs can be used.

- Young children need clear lessons in taking turns and sharing – simple games like rolling a ball to and fro with one child initially and then extending the game to more children in a small group. When playing a game, show and tell the child clearly what the rules are and play with them until you feel they are aware of the rules.

- As soon as young children appear to be aware of rules, leave them when minor squabbles arise and only intervene if the situation becomes difficult.

- Be careful that you do not offer too many choices to a young child. Simple choices like 'We are going to visit Aunty Mary today. Do you want your blue or red socks on?' enable a child to become accustomed to making minor choices. This gives the child the satisfaction of making a choice. Generally a selection of two items should be offered until the child has matured sufficiently to make greater choices.

Good practice in seven simple steps

1. Be consistent.

2. Use praise and rewards.

3. Provide good models.

4. Guide the child.

5. Ignore bad behaviour.

6. Remove from the scene.

7. Apply sanctions.

STEP 1
BE CONSISTENT

Start as you mean to go on and be calm, clear and consistent. Remaining calm and not 'mirroring' the behaviour of a child is a useful tactic when dealing with children who are, for example, having a temper tantrum. Reacting to attention-seeking behaviours in a cool, deliberate manner will have the effect of showing that you are displeased while not giving the child the kind of heightened attention he is seeking. If a child is throwing construction toys for instance, the adult might simply walk up to him, very quietly remind him of the rules and swiftly withdraw the toy as a consequence.

Once the rules in your setting have been established and all staff members know how to deal with certain behaviours, it is vital that everyone responds in the same way. It is very difficult to backtrack once a precedent has been set. For example, if throwing sand is allowed to go unchecked one day, it will encourage children to keep testing the boundaries. As long as everyone knows the rules and how they are to be applied, it will be much easier to be consistent. Children feel secure when they know and understand what the rules are and what is expected of them.

STEP 2
USE PRAISE AND REWARDS

This is the most effective way of reinforcing good behaviour. Always reward the child who tries, to show that he is succeeding and that succeeding is fun. Show the child how pleased you are.

Rewards can be all sorts of things – praise, hugs, smiles, stickers, stars, smiley faces, favourite activities, computer time, reading stories together, choosing time, certificates, etc. How do you decide which to use? Using rewards is very much up to each individual setting. In some settings, it is policy to use only verbal rewards and to acknowledge rather than to praise wanted behaviours. Some children particularly like certain rewards, for example being allowed extra time at a favourite activity, or a 'well done' sticker on their T-shirt. One of the most effective rewards is adult praise or acknowledgement. A simple 'I really liked the way you helped Jack to carry all those toys to the cupboard' can be very effective. Recognizing achievements publicly is a powerful tool for raising self-esteem and motivation. Rewards do not have to be 'big' to have the desired effect. Varying rewards and changing them when they lose impact is important for maintaining motivation; one type of reward does not necessarily fit all children.

Five simple rules for rewards

1. Reward should be immediate: for example, if Jack has in the past been reluctant to tidy up and he is spotted helping to put things away, you could IMMEDIATELY say something like 'Thank you Jack for doing such a good job and making things so tidy.'
2. Reward every time at first and less often when the child finds it easier. If the same reward is given when a child has become better at performing a particular task, the impact is lost. This will have the effect of diminishing motivation on the child's part.
3. Always praise the child when giving rewards.
4. Always say exactly why you're pleased with him. Instead of 'good boy' or 'well done', say 'I liked the way you waited for Luke to get off the slide before you went down. That was very sensible and grown-up.'
5. Reward children for all different types of good behaviour, so that every child has a chance of being rewarded (see p. 8 for ideas).

Praise

Use the child's name when praising him for doing the right thing. Children who behave badly often hear their names called out (their surnames too sometimes) but well-behaved children can go for days without hearing their name spoken out loud. If you see someone doing something helpful try saying, 'Well done, Kayleigh. That was very kind of you/that looks very neat/etc.' Some children really like to hear their name called for doing the right thing, and this may help to reduce the number of instances of bad behaviour. It also lessens the likelihood that children will be labelled 'naughty Tommy' (to distinguish him from 'reasonably well-behaved Tommy' and 'always well-behaved Tommy').

Positive and specific comments

When praising a child for doing the right thing it is important that he knows exactly what he has done right! Just saying 'Well done, Jamilla' may well mystify some children (especially if they had just done something naughty that you missed). It is far more effective to say, for example, 'Well done, Jamilla, for sitting up so nicely,' or 'Well done, Philip, for lining up so sensibly,' as this will give a much clearer message not only to the target child but also to others standing nearby. Note: children with very low self-esteem sometimes find any kind of praise hard to handle. There can be occasions when adults have commented enthusiastically on a child's painting only to find two minutes later that they have scribbled all over it with black paint. These children need very sensitive handling and may respond better if you praise a couple of children together, for example 'Well done you two for painting such colourful pictures,' or 'Well done all of you who are playing in the sand so sensibly.'

Children can easily miss comments made to them, or questions asked of them, especially if they are engaged in an activity. Saying their name first will alert them: 'Rory ... Well done, you are getting on really well with your work. Michael ... Why do you think the baby bear was crying?'

We can praise and reward children for:

- sharing;

- turn-taking;

- tidying up;

- washing paint pots;

- taking a message;

- helping a friend;

- showing kindness;

- asking a good question;

- giving a good answer;

- putting on their own coat;

- remembering to bring something from home;

- noticing something interesting;

- having a good idea;

- being sensible;

- being brave;

- being patient.

STEP 3
PROVIDE GOOD MODELS

Point out to the child someone who is doing well. Praise that person and encourage the child to do the same. Always try to show the child the behaviours you want by commenting when other children are doing the right thing: 'I can see someone sitting very still, listening carefully and looking at me. Well done, Sara.'

When sharing stories, use the characters to share ideas with the child about good and bad behaviour: 'What do you think about Roger not taking his turn to help set the table?' (*It's Your Turn, Roger!* by Susanna Gretz published by Red Box).

Use the home corner to model good behaviour: 'Thank you for the cup of tea, Ben. You have been so kind to me. Let me do the washing up for you.'

Use puppets to demonstrate good and bad behaviour: 'Susan was very naughty to take the biscuit from Teddy. Teddy is crying now and doesn't want to play with her any more. Let's bring on Kind Kelly to show Susan how to share with friends. Kelly has lots of friends – why do you think everyone likes to play with her?'

STEP 4
GUIDE THE CHILD

For example when clearing away, show the child step by step and expect him to do it in a similar sequence: 'Well done, Tom, you've sorted out the wax crayons from the pencils. Now let's put the crayons into the red box and the pencils into the tub. Then we can put everything away in the cupboard.'

Help the child to succeed by breaking up tasks into smaller, achievable steps, and praise at each stage. For example, if a child has difficulty sharing toys and pushes others away when they attempt to play, you could at first only expect him to play a simple interactive game such as rolling a ball to another child with adult supervision and then perhaps gradually increase the time and numbers in the group. By introducing different activities and turn-taking in a very small group at first and rewarding each success, you can build upon achievements in a positive manner.

Giving a child take-up time can also help. If you ask a child to do something, particularly if it is something they do not really want to do, it helps if you do not stand over him and watch. Give him some space and take-up time and he may well comply without your even having to repeat the instruction. A really big egg-timer can also help when you want a particular activity to stop. Advance warning of changes of activity is beneficial in reducing conflict, for example: 'When the sand has gone through I would like you all to be sitting on the carpet/ have your coats on.'

When choosing is required, use limited choices such as 'Would you like to play with Lego or the cars?' If too many choices are presented it could encourage lack of focus and 'flitting'. The most difficult times of the day/session for children with behavioural difficulties are the unstructured times, for example free choice and outdoor play. It is during these particular times that the child will need the most direction and support. You could try helping him to plan for himself what he wants to do first – explain the choices and remind him exactly how you expect him to behave: 'We are going outside now, Simon. You could ride on the trike or play on the slide – which one will you choose? If you play on the trike, remember to go round the other children so that you don't bump into them. If you play on the slide, you have to let other children have a go as well, so climb up the steps and slide down when it's your turn. If you stand on the steps all the time, the other children can't have a go.' You may need to repeat the expectation once Simon has chosen his activity and is actually on the equipment.

Plan what you will do with a child who finds it very difficult to move about the setting in an appropriate way. If you are moving from one room to another, support the child by having an adult walking next to him giving prompts or even holding his hand, and modelling the expected behaviour. Praise him if the behaviour is achieved.

STEP 5
IGNORE BAD BEHAVIOUR

Ignore irritating behaviour whenever possible and always try to avoid confrontation. It is often best to ignore the child's behaviour if it is annoying but not too severe, for example a child constantly calling out. Ignoring means not giving any attention and pretending the behaviour is not affecting you at all. Make it clear to the child before the story time or circle time session that he will have a special reward when the story or circle time is finished if he has managed to sit quietly. (Be warned that initially the child's behaviour is likely to become worse as he struggles even harder to get what he wants, especially if he is seeking attention. You have to ignore him every time and make sure he doesn't receive attention from anyone else.)

Tactical ignoring can also avoid drawing everyone's attention to the unwanted behaviour. For instance, if a child is quietly staring into space and not following your instructions, there is no point in saying, 'Stop daydreaming, David.' All that happens then is that everyone near David stops what they are doing to look at him and instead of one child off task you have a whole group. A far more effective strategy is to say, 'Well done, Leah and Daisy, for tidying up.' Quite often Leah and Daisy will tidy up even more quickly and happily and with luck, David will stop daydreaming and help too. Similarly, giving out some new crayons or pencils to a group of children actively engaged in a task can be a real incentive to others to settle down and join in.

A lot of children react badly to the word 'No' and have learnt that engaging adults in a lengthy argument will often result in the adult giving in for the sake of a quiet life (the alternative being a major wobbly at the checkout!). By saying 'Yes, when …', rather than 'No, because …' you can reduce the likelihood of confrontation. For example, if a child wants to play with the Lego but needs to wash the paint off his hands first, try saying, 'Yes, when you've washed your hands, then you can play with the Lego' rather than 'No, because you've got dirty hands.'

Similarly, if a child is in the wrong place doing the wrong thing, for example splashing others by the sink rather than sitting listening to a story, try asking him, 'What are you supposed to be doing?' rather than 'Why are you doing that?' 'Why?' questions tend to get in response either a blank stare, one of those irritating shoulder shrugs or an obviously true answer such as 'Because I like splashing water around.' The 'What are you supposed to be doing?' question or 'Can you remember what I asked you to do?' should elicit a more suitable answer.

STEP 6
REMOVE FROM THE SCENE

Removing the child from the situation and giving him some 'time out' can prevent escalation of the problem and allow him a 'cooling off' time out of sight of the other children. As always, announce 'time out' in a calm voice and reserve it for more serious misdemeanours such as aggression, violence, destructiveness or repeated rudeness.

Time out should be for the minimum possible time – a few minutes are as effective as a longer period. A useful guide is to consider the age of the child. A three-year-old could have a three-minute time-out period. An egg timer could be used to measure this. It should not be a humiliating or scary experience for the child but more a chance to calm down and return to the room to make a fresh start, hopefully with an apology if this is appropriate. Someone should stay with the child and sit close to him, but be careful not to reward with an activity he likes doing or making him too comfy in the staffroom for example. Think carefully about what to call the time-out place: the 'peaceful cushion', or the 'quiet place' or the 'calming corner' has more positive connotations than the 'naughty corner'!

STEP 7
APPLY SANCTIONS

Use sanctions only as a last resort. Taking away privileges such as choosing time or a special activity can be powerful in making a point with a child, but may well be counter-productive if he feels embittered about it. With children whose parents frequently use sanctions as a punishment, the impact will be minimal. If you do decide to take this route, make sure the child remembers why this is happening, especially if there has been a time lapse: 'Darren,  you won't be having a go on the computer today because you kicked Iqbal and made him cry. I know you like to play on the computer so I hope you will be kind to everyone in nursery tomorrow and then you can have your turn.'

Remember – rewards are much more effective than sanctions so **catch the child being good**.

SOME ADDITIONAL IDEAS

Noise levels

Many children have only two settings on their volume control – VERY LOUD and EVEN LOUDER. Letting off steam and shouting while playing outdoors is very different from doing the same thing indoors with lots of others; some children will need to be shown the difference between an indoor voice and a playground or outdoor voice. It is vital that the adults also demonstrate the difference and refrain from shouting across the room to each other or talking to each other while everyone is supposed to be watching a video for example. A **noisometer** could be positioned on the wall (like a thermometer) with a movable arrow that can be pointed to 'Just Right', 'Getting a Bit Loud' and 'Far Too Noisy'. A traffic light indicator might also be used. One successful strategy is to use a puppet or soft toy which goes into hiding if it gets too noisy and only comes out for a cuddle when things have quietened down again. This seems to work for all ages of children.

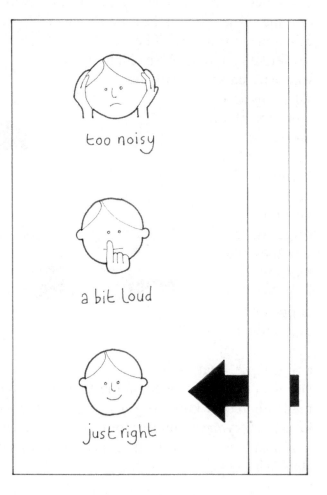

NOISOMETER

too noisy

a bit loud

just right

Chairs

If you are reading a story with the children sitting on the carpet in front of you it is very tempting to tell a fidgety child who is getting on everyone's nerves to go and sit on a chair. Although this gets him out of the situation and stops him irritating others, there is a fundamental problem with this strategy. By giving the badly behaved child a chair to sit on – which, let's face it, is a lot more comfortable than sitting on a hard floor – we can be seen to be rewarding unwanted behaviour. Try giving the child his own 'sitting spot', a square of carpet or material or a chalk-drawn shape.

Be alert to children becoming uncomfortable – allow them to get up, move about, have a stretch then settle down again. Young children should not be expected to sit still for long periods of time – it's difficult enough for adults!

Playing outdoors

Some children are reasonably well behaved indoors but get completely out of hand in more open spaces, barging into others and spoiling their games. It may be worth considering some form of 'passport' which they give to the outside supervisor, who puts a smiley face on the passport if they have a good playtime. Five smiley faces result in a special certificate, star or choice of favourite activity. Teaching children how to play simple games can help with problems like this (Oranges and Lemons, Old Macdonald, What's the Time Mr Wolf?) and getting them to run round (all the same way) for a few minutes helps to burn off excess energy.

Rules

If your setting has some clearly displayed and easily understood rules you can save a lot of unnecessary dialogue by simply repeating the rule. If a child is swearing or shouting, rather than admonishing him you can say: 'We speak kindly,' or 'We play carefully and safely.'

In brief:

- Make sure rules are known and understood by the children, parents and all staff – revisit them often.

- Use a home–school liaison book for positive behaviours/achievements to share with parents/carers and in the setting.

- Use a high degree of structure for children with behaviour problems.

- Give responsibility to children with behavioural difficulties, for example by appointing them as the helper at snack time.

- Use favourite activities as rewards.

- Use visual aids wherever possible, e.g. if giving instructions about washing hands, show a picture of the children using the wash area.

- Use a personal carpet square or 'spot' for children who have problems sitting still for a story.

- Use a variety of rewards and change them when they lose impact.

- Use extension activities – keep a box of resources ready and add to it over time.

- Make sure children know what you mean if you have to tell them off. 'Stop that' is not enough – 'Stop throwing sand' will send the message to all the children.

- Following a request, say 'thank you'; this implies that the request will be carried out.

Quick tips for establishing good relationships

- Be positive and generous with praise.

- Be careful how you talk to people. It is much better to say 'You will find it easier if …' rather than 'Don't do it like that.' Remember, an unkind word lingers much longer than a kind one.

- Label the act NOT the child, e.g. 'Pushing Fred was a dangerous thing to do,' rather than 'YOU are a bully.' Negative labels stick.

- Build in success. Make sure that programmes of work enable all children to succeed in some way.

- Think back. Remember your own schooldays? Teachers are the creators of memories – make sure that your setting is a happy one. Do not be afraid to have some fun.

- Smile. Non-verbal messages are important to children. A pat on the back, a smile, a nod gives as much encouragement as words.

- Children often have the answer. After an incident, ask the child, 'Why might I be angry now?' Encourage children to analyse their own behaviour and begin to take responsibility for it.

Quick tips for raising self-esteem

- Celebrate children's differences and unique personalities – don't expect every child to behave/respond in the same way.

- Find something to praise in every child, every day.

- Look at every child – establish eye contact as often as possible.

- Make time to listen to children as well as talk to them.

- Take their feelings seriously by noticing and acknowledging feelings whether good or bad.

Things to say
'I expect you are feeling … now.'
'That must be upsetting … do you want to tell me about it?'
'You seem …'
'You look …'

Real children in real settings: behaviours that cause concern and strategies for coping

CASE STUDY 1

A quiet, withdrawn child

William spends much of his time at pre-school in the book area on his own. He watches the other children but will not respond when they try to talk to him. He hides his face and looks the other way when children try to talk and play with him. Most children now leave him on his own.

Possible reasons for this behaviour:

- shyness – it may be a part of William's personality;
- does William get attention at home for this behaviour?;
- difficulty with understanding language;
- difficulty with social skills; William may not have had a lot of social contact before joining pre-school and needs time to adjust to a busy environment;
- withdrawn behaviour may indicate some more serious underlying problems at home if it persists over several weeks in spite of appropriate responses by staff.

Strategies:

- Avoid pressurising him – he may need time to settle and just watch for a while, joining in when he is ready.
- Talk with parents/carers and find out how William behaves at home. A home visit can often tell you a great deal.
- Check that his hearing is not impaired.
- Encourage William to play with one child initially, alongside each other with Lego (or similar). Gradually introduce some co-operative element such as building a fort together.
- Monitor William's behaviour when on his own or when encouraged by an adult, to find out what he enjoys doing.
- Praise him whenever he is with other children.
- Introduce a 'special friend' for the day who will help William to join in with activities.
- (Add your own ideas here).

CASE STUDY 2

A child demanding constant adult attention

As soon as Tara comes into pre-school she seeks an adult and will not leave her mother until she is holding the hand of another adult. She will only play or do activities when an adult is near her, and constantly looks out for adults. Whenever she does a puzzle she looks at the adult before she puts the pieces in the slots. When the adult moves away she will just sit and do nothing or watch for the adult coming back.

Possible reasons for this behaviour:

- Coming into a new environment and feeling insecure is the primary reason for this sort of behaviour. It is important to be patient and allow enough time for children to feel at home with new surroundings and unfamiliar people;
- Adults at home have done most things for her and not encouraged independence;
- She is the youngest in the family, where she is treated as 'the baby', and wants to maintain this level of attention;
- Receptive language difficulties – not understanding what adults are saying and therefore unsure about what she should be doing.

Strategies:

- Find out about the family situation and try to work out a simple plan to encourage independence at home. For example, the first emphasis could be on Tara attempting to do a puzzle or play with a toy by herself. She should be praised every time an adult notices her trying to do this on her own.
- Implement an intensive praise and reinforcement schedule so that Tara begins to recognize all the good things she is doing. Initially it will be important to praise Tara for every single thing she attempts and draw her attention to the way she is progressing. In this way she will gain self-confidence.

- Design a specific programme for Tara coming into the pre-school. When she is greeted by an adult worker she could then be introduced to another child and the two children could be encouraged to play with something they enjoy or to share a story together.
- Work out a simple recording system so that Tara and her parents/carers become aware of how she is progressing. A simple star or sticker chart will serve as a record of how many times Tara has tried to do things on her own – but be aware that stickers do not work as a reward for *all* children.

CASE STUDY 3

A child who screams when asked to participate in an adult-led activity

Most of the time, Kieran really enjoys pre-school. He is a lively boy with lots of friends and loves the big equipment such as the slides and scooters. He is very happy playing with things he enjoys. The problem starts when he is asked to do some table-top activities. He starts to scream really loudly so that many children stop what they are doing. This can go on for about 15 minutes.

Possible reasons for this behaviour:

- This is learnt behaviour from home – if he screams for long enough he will get what he wants;
- He is attention-seeking and knows that if he screams people will watch him;
- He has difficulty with some table-top activities and does not like seeing other children doing things better than him. He is afraid of failure. He has difficulties with following instructions.

Strategies:

- Remove any audience if possible and ensure the other children are engaged in their own activities. If you have an area or another room available, move the other children away, leaving one adult to watch over Kieran.
- Encourage Kieran to sit in a quiet area until he is ready to join in. This needs to be explained to him before any screaming sessions start so that he is aware that he can have some time to think about what he is doing.
- Use a visual timetable so that Kieran can choose his own activities for the session but ensure that he understands that he must include at least one table-top activity. In this way he is becoming involved in making his own choices but with the understanding that it includes a range of activities.
- Use a visual timetable on which the order of events is clearly displayed. Kieran can then finish each section before moving on to the next section.
- Reward him on any occasion that he does co-operate with table-top activities.

CASE STUDY 4

A child who kicks children and adults

Dominic enjoys the big toys at pre-school. He likes the slide and playing chasing games with two other boys. If he is asked to come along to a table-top activity and he does not want to, he will kick out at the pre-school worker and refuse to go. If he wants to play with a particular toy and other children will not let him, he will kick those children and also bite them. He has been known to bite adults.

Possible reasons for this behaviour:

- Dominic has learned that he gets to do things he wants to when he kicks and bites;
- Dominic has had no models of sharing and insufficient positive experience of sharing;
- He does not consider the feelings of others and finds it difficult to respond to meaningful social situations.

Strategies:

- Dominic will need praise whenever he plays well with other children and responds to adult requests. ('Well done, Dominic, I like the way you waited for Sean to get off the trike – isn't he kind to let you have a go.')
- There will need to be clear rules in place at pre-school so that Dominic is fully aware of expectations of his behaviour. These rules will need to include how to relate to other children when they are playing with toys and how to ask them politely if he wants to play with a toy they have. Some stories and (puppet) role-play may prove useful.
- Dominic will need to learn that kicking and biting is unacceptable behaviour, and clear consequences should be in place for when he does bite or kick. It will be important that he does not receive additional adult attention for his biting or kicking.

- Dominic may benefit from specific sessions to teach social skills such as turn-taking and sharing equipment. These could be carried out in small groups focusing on a specific theme, such as when a child wants to play with a toy that someone else has. Role-play would be helpful.
- Keep pointing out children who are playing nicely and who are able to share toys so that Dominic becomes fully aware of what is expected of him.

CASE STUDY 5

A child with a very short attention span

Rehanah cannot sit still and listen to a story at story time. She constantly shuffles about on her hands and knees, disturbing the children around her. She does not seem to notice that other children are trying to listen to the story. She constantly shouts out and interrupts the story and tries to talk about irrelevant things.

Possible reasons for this behaviour:

- little experience of listening to stories and group situations;
- hearing difficulties;
- attention-seeking;
- receptive language problems: understanding of language. Rehanah may not understand every word in a sentence when being spoken to; she may only understand one or two key words, making stories very difficult to follow;
- social awareness difficulties: Rehanah may have difficulty with the social rules of behaviour, e.g. not butting in when others are talking;
- very immature behaviour, which could be a reflection of her general cognitive abilities.

Strategies:

- Give her a special place to sit, such as on a cushion, and let her hold a special toy so that 'Teddy' can listen to the story too. Initially, expect Rehanah to sit for a short length of time such as three minutes with an adult nearby. Gradually the time can be extended and the adult can move farther away. If she manages to sit still for the required time, give her a reward.
- Suggest to her parents/carers that they arrange for an eye test and/or hearing test via the GP. If the behaviour continues despite clear expectations and a carefully structured behaviour plan, it may be helpful for her to sit near an adult reading the story so that she can see the pictures more clearly or be more involved in the process by helping to turn the pages over. In this way she will be given special responsibility and can be praised.

- Give praise whenever Rehanah is sitting still and looks as if she is listening, so that she receives attention whenever she is being 'good'. She may need to be shown very clearly what 'being good' is. When possible, ignore her shuffling.
- Point out children who are sitting nicely and listening so that Rehanah is clear about expectations. It can be helpful to remind children before the story of the way to listen: 'Bottoms on the floor, lips together, eyes looking at me' – with appropriate gestures. Try asking them a specific question at the beginning. In this way they are listening out for something specific in the story-telling.
- Let Rehanah become accustomed to listening to stories by sitting in a small group or one-to-one with an adult so that she gets used to listening to the whole story. Start with very short stories. Stories recorded on tape and heard through headphones can be useful.
- Praise her whenever you see her sitting still.
- Have a clear system in place for whenever Rehanah is causing disruption such as sitting her on her own away from the group with a book.
- Use a real photograph (with parents' permission) of Rehanah sitting still to act as a prompt: 'Look, Rehanah, here you are sitting very still. I hope you will be sitting like this while I read the story today.'
- Monitor her rate of learning. If she has difficulty in naming colours, learning simple rhymes, constructing simple phrases, the inattentive behaviour may be part of a general learning difficulty.

CASE STUDY 6

A child who has temper tantrums

Danny finds change very difficult to handle and can suddenly explode if asked to stop what he is doing. In the past few days this has become of serious concern and he has kicked adults and children when asked to stop throwing sand around the room.

Possible reasons for this behaviour:

- change of circumstances at home, making him unsettled;
- his age – lack of maturity;
- change of circumstances at pre-school;
- medical – is he in pain/not feeling well?;
- autistic spectrum disorder.

Strategies:

- Give warnings about changes to routine or activity at 5–10 minute intervals so Danny begins to start thinking about doing something different.
- Explain beforehand about expected behaviour.
- Make consequences very clear.
- Use a visual timetable and make it personal with prompts if needed.
- Ask Danny directly why he is behaving as he is – what is bothering him?
- Reassure him.

CASE STUDY 7

A child who is oppositional

Rajinder frequently refuses point blank to comply with the most reasonable of requests, e.g. 'Come and join us in the story corner.' She sits on the floor with her head down and refuses to make eye contact. She will keep this up for an hour or more. If attempts are made to move her she will cling to the leg of a table.

Possible reasons for this behaviour:

- social communication problems;
- serious problems within the family;
- difficulties in understanding the social organization of the pre-school, e.g. there may be a lack of experience of social groups. Rajinder may never have had contact with large groups of children and adults who are not part of her family;
- there could be cultural differences that Rajinder finds unfamiliar;
- language comprehension difficulties: there may be undetected speech and language problems associated with processing language and understanding what is being said.

Strategies:

- Ask parents/carers if they know why she is behaving like this.
- Arrange for speech and language assessment (see *Early Years Action Plus*, p. 90).
- Suggest to parents/carers that they arrange a hearing assessment via their GP.
- Introduce a buddy system so that another child steers her in the right direction.
- Find out what she enjoys doing at home, and bring into pre-school.
- Use a visual timetable so she becomes aware of the structure of the day.
- Where possible, give her a choice, e.g. 'Rajinder, would you like to sit next to me in the story corner, or next to Simon?' 'Would you like to join us in the story corner, or look at a book by yourself?'
- Give a warning when activities are going to stop, e.g. 'In two minutes' time when you hear the rain stick, we are going to tidy up.'

CASE STUDY 8

A child who refuses to talk (selective mute)

Andy appears to understand what is being said to him and will join in most activities. He will not, however, speak to anyone, adult or child, in the pre-school setting. His mother reports that he chats away merrily at home.

Possible reasons for this behaviour:

- Andy uses this as a controlling mechanism;
- Fear of failure – it could be safer not to talk;
- He may be intimidated by some/all children in the setting.

Strategies:

- Never try to 'force' Andy to speak or draw attention to his unwillingness to speak.
- Suggest someone from home comes to the pre-school to talk to Andy so that he can speak with someone familiar while in the setting.
- Ensure there are some non-verbal systems in place (e.g. PECS, see 'Useful addresses').
- Be prepared to be patient over a long period.
- Use puppets as a method of communicating.
- After a period of time, if things do not improve, Andy may need some professional help via *Early Years Action Plus* (see p. 90).

CASE STUDY 9

A child who is unable to share

Peter will not share anything; he snatches toys out of the hands of other children and has been known to take small objects home (pieces of Lego etc.) hidden in his pockets.

Possible reasons for this behaviour:

- his age – immaturity;
- possible low self-esteem;
- deprived circumstances in the home;
- insecurity;
- seeking attention.

Strategies:

- Explain clearly where items and equipment should be put after use.
- Ask Peter why he likes to take things home. Is there a toy library he could use? Are there any story sacks he could take home?
- Make a 'borrowing bag' for Peter – allow him to borrow books and toys overnight but insist that he brings them back the next day. Enlist the cooperation of parents/carers for this sort of arrangement.
- Try to raise self-esteem by pointing out achievements and using praise.
- Talk to his parents/carers about Peter's habit of putting objects into his pockets, but make absolutely sure that there is no doubt about what he is doing.
- Never 'search' Peter for lost objects or automatically assume that he has taken something that is missing.

CASE STUDY 10

A child who has difficulty turn-taking

Sarah has a favourite toy and likes to play with this every day. Whenever there is a choice, she will monopolize the train set. If another child attempts to join her or even just to play alongside, she will respond by pushing the child away and become agitated if her space is invaded. Sarah will also refuse to wait her turn during games in small-group situations, often demanding to start first.

Possible reasons for this behaviour:

- insecurity;
- anxiety;
- inability to empathize with others;
- over-indulgence/used to getting own way at home, possibly the youngest/only child;
- lack of maturity;
- she may not have a train set at home and particularly likes it;
- she feels comfortable playing in that particular section of the pre-school.

Strategies:

- temporary removal of train set from the room;
- encouraging a short game with an adult, then one other child and an adult to model appropriate behaviour and gradually increase the group numbers;
- instant praise for appropriate behaviour;
- use of train set as a reward – set aside special times for Sarah to play with the train;
- clear explanation of expectations on a session basis;
- pairing up with buddy role model;
- use of a visual prop to signal 'it's your turn' – only a child wearing the special tunic/hat/arm band can play with the train.

CASE STUDY 11

A child who may have autistic spectrum disorder (ASD)

Michael seems withdrawn and appears to lack ability to interact with others in the expected manner. He is mostly quiet and content to occupy himself with an activity of his own choosing, when he displays the ability to concentrate for long periods. He will scream in a high-pitched voice when he feels thwarted and will sometimes refuse to join an adult-led activity and will rock to and fro. When Michael is playing he will often make flapping movements with his hands. He dislikes the routine being changed and becomes distressed whenever this happens.

Possible reasons for this behaviour:

- experience of trauma;
- neglect in the home;
- autistic spectrum disorder;
- language disorder.

Strategies:

- Introduce a high degree of structure to the day.
- Use a personal, pictorial timetable for Michael.
- Take care to use unambiguous language.
- Give simple instructions accompanied by visual aids.
- Allow time for Michael to 'process' instructions.
- Use direct teaching of appropriate behaviours.
- Make clear rules and boundaries.
- Give very clear explanation of any changes to routine and assurances about when it will end, e.g. if going out for a walk always tell him that you will be coming back to the nursery/school.
- Ignore behaviours such as hand flapping or the insistence of wearing hats/hoods etc. (if the behaviour is not hurting the child or others – ignore).

CASE STUDY 12

A child who is aggressive

Bhupinder likes to behave to her own agenda. She refuses to share equipment and monopolizes her favourite things. If another child approaches her at the sand tray, she often responds with verbal aggression and will throw sand into the child's face. She has a history of hitting other children and consequently they avoid contact with her.

Possible reasons for this behaviour:

- immaturity;
- poor language skills;
- poor role models, experience of aggression in the home;
- lack of experience in social skills;
- low self-esteem.

Strategies:

- use of personalized positive reinforcement every time appropriate behaviours are observed.
- temporary removal of sand tray.
- use of rules and consequences.
- tactical ignoring of inappropriate behaviours.
- modelling of good and bad behaviour, e.g. with stories and puppets.
- home–school contact book for positive comments.
- involvement of the child in evaluating her own behaviour, e.g. use of smiley faces.

CASE STUDY 13

A child who scribbles on other children's drawings

Jack will often scribble all over the drawings of children nearby during art activities.

Possible reasons for this behaviour:

- low self-esteem – worries that other children's work is better than his own;
- attention-seeking – may enjoy the reaction of adults and children following this behaviour;
- lack of social experiences;
- lack of empathy with others.

Strategies:

- Raise self-esteem by highlighting achievements.
- Provide close supervision during drawing activities: talk to Jack about his picture and help him to stay focused.
- Allow him to change to a different activity as soon as he loses interest in drawing.
- Ignore negative behaviours.
- Pair up with appropriate role model.
- Make expectations very clear.

CASE STUDY 14

A child who scribbles on her own drawings

After completing a drawing/painting Tracey will often scribble all over the picture with a black or red crayon.

Possible reasons for this behaviour:

- She may just enjoy the sensation of colouring over the picture;
- She is upset by home circumstances;
- Low self-esteem – she may feel that her work is not good enough.

Strategies:

- Check with parents/carers that this is her usual behaviour at home – ask them whether anything is worrying Tracey.
- Very prominently display a picture which has not been scribbled over, and praise her for it.
- If Tracey uses a lot of red or black colouring materials, ask parents/carers to check the possibility of colour blindness.
- Monitor closely and seek the help of an educational psychologist via *Early Years Action Plus* if the behaviour persists (see p. 90).

CASE STUDY 15

A child who constantly says 'No'

Jordan has a strong temperament and enjoys pre-school when he can do activities he likes. If he is asked to go to a table-top activity he just keeps saying 'No, I won't go. You can't make me. I'll tell my mum,' over and over again. He will not move but just keeps saying the words.

Possible reasons for this behaviour:

- He has learnt the behaviour from home or elsewhere;
- He finds table-top activities difficult and is more confident in other areas;
- He likes to control, wants to have the last word;
- He has learnt that he will get his own way if he carries on for long enough;
- He feels insecure and this is his way of keeping a grip on things.

Strategies:

- Tactical ignoring – give no attention but immediately go to another child. It is important that Jordan is not allowed to carry on with other activities but has to stay in a set place until he is ready to join in the set activity – this will have to be planned by all staff.
- Give Jordan a restricted choice of activity: 'Do you want to do some cutting out on this table or play a matching game over on that table?'
- Continue with Jordan as if you have not heard, and gently lead him to the activity table.
- Use a timetable with Jordan so that he is aware of which activities he will need to do during the session – he can agree these and they can be recorded simply. He can cross out the activity as he completes it.
- Discuss with parents/carers so that similar ideas can be carried out at home if this is possible.
- Give praise whenever Jordan is doing what is expected.

CASE STUDY 16

A child who makes himself sick

Gerry's parents have become very concerned as he is often sick before coming to pre-school. His parents still bring him and he usually settles. During the sessions he will often say he feels sick and rushes to the toilet and stays there for quite a long time on occasions. Gerry has been sent home in the past but his mother reports that he is fine as soon as he gets home.

Possible reasons for this behaviour:

- He is a highly anxious child who does not like change;
- Has there been a change of family circumstances such as a new baby?
- Gerry has learnt that if he says he feels sick, adults will give a high level of attention;
- Dietary problems, e.g. intolerance to certain foods;
- Medical reasons;
- Gerry finds it difficult to manage the complex social structure of a pre-school setting;
- He is very attached to his mother;
- Gerry may feel that his mother is upset and wants him to stay at home.

Strategies:

- Talk to Gerry about all the interesting things happening at the pre-school and encourage Mum to do the same before setting out from home.
- Recognize that Gerry may be a very anxious child and talk more with him about other children not wanting to leave their mother – he needs to be made aware that other children feel the same. Use stories/puppets.
- Provide Gerry with a key worker who greets him in the mornings and to whom he can go at any time during the session.

- Gerry may not have the language to express how he feels. It can be useful for adults to try to support him in verbalising his thoughts by saying such things as 'I think you like to play here but like to be with your mum as well.' Both parents and pre-school staff need to give the same message and reassure Gerry that his worries will lessen each day.
- Check out any medical reasons for the difficulties.
- Consider whether he has difficulties in understanding what is said to him (receptive language problems).
- It is more helpful if pre-school staff can work out ways of keeping Gerry at pre-school rather than sending him home.

CASE STUDY 17

A child who runs out of the room

Brandon is a lively boy and enjoys the big equipment and large space at the pre-school. He has worked out how to open the door and runs out of the large hall whenever possible. He also watches for staff as they open the door and will try to run out then.

Possible reasons for this behaviour:

- Brandon sees this as a game;
- He gets attention for doing this;
- He is curious about what is happening outside the hall;
- Brandon does not feel sufficiently 'confined' in such a large hall;
- He does this at home or elsewhere and he enjoys being chased by adults;
- Brandon is not ready for a full pre-school session;
- He is not sufficiently involved in/challenged by the activities on offer.

Strategies:

- Take Brandon on a tour of the building so that his curiosity is satisfied.
- Plan some special games and activities that will engage him.
- Give Brandon a high level of attention when he is focused on activities in the hall.
- Think about sectioning off the large hall into smaller areas if possible.
- Use going out of the large hall as a special reward for completing other activities – Brandon's reward could be to go for a five-minute walk outside the hall with an adult.
- Ask Brandon what he thinks might be outside of the hall and why he likes to go out.
- Discuss with parents/carers the possibility of shortening the session at pre-school until Brandon is ready for a longer session.
- Agree with parents/carers about what will happen when Brandon runs out.

CASE STUDY 18

A child who hides under the table

Chantelle is generally a quiet girl at nursery and seems to enjoy being there for most of the time. Members of staff are concerned as she hides under a table regularly, tucks herself in a corner and just stays there and will not come out.

Possible reasons for this behaviour:

- Chantelle finds the lively atmosphere too difficult;
- There are difficult circumstances at home that are upsetting her;
- She gets tired quickly;
- She needs time for personal space;
- She needs the security of a smaller, more comforting area.

Strategies:

- Give Chantelle a special quiet place to go in the nursery or allow her to sit/lie on a cushion under the table.
- Discuss with parents/carers whether they know why this is happening – does this happen at home?
- Encourage her to have a buddy who will sit with her in a quiet area.
- Think about the structure of the session – are there enough quiet times or quiet areas where Chantelle can go?
- Organize a timetable for Chantelle so that there are opportunities for her to have a quiet time during the sessions.

CASE STUDY 19

A child who self-injures

Tariq is a mischievous little boy and generally likes to join in with most pre-school activities. On occasions he just will not join in and will head-butt against the wall or the floor if staff try to encourage him to join in.

Possible reasons for this behaviour:

- Tariq does not like to join in with specific activities;
- He has not learnt a more appropriate way of saying he does not want to join in at that time;
- He may be experiencing some pain, such as earache, or there may be another medical reason;
- He has learnt that this method will get him his own way at home.

Strategies:

- Identify the 'trigger points' for this behaviour and consider whether they can be avoided.
- Tariq will need to be taught alternative ways of saying he does not wish to do something – it may be helpful for staff to verbalize how they think he is feeling, saying something like, 'I think that it makes you feel angry/annoyed/cross when I ask you to sit at the art table.'
- Tactical ignoring. Ensure that Tariq cannot hurt himself – he should be placed in an area with cushions while staff observe him from a distance.
- Provide visual communication cards to help him communicate how he is feeling (simple illustration).
- Ask parent/carers to check out any medical reasons if that is felt to be a useful route.
- Tariq will require a lot of praise when he is doing things well.
- Although it can be very frightening for adults to watch, most children who use this tactic as a method of control know their limits and will not seriously hurt themselves.

CASE STUDY 20

A child who swears

Storm has recently started at pre-school and constantly swears at staff and children. This swearing can last several minutes and be highly repetitive. Storm does not speak very much apart from the swearing.

Possible reasons for this behaviour:

- Storm has learnt vocabulary from home or elsewhere;
- She is not aware of the social inappropriateness of such language;
- She may get attention at home for swearing and continues with that in the pre-school;
- Language disorder and difficulty, e.g. Tourette's syndrome or neurological problems (this is rare);
- She may use swear words at home if she does not want to do something.

Strategies:

- Storm may need to be taught alternative words to use at pre-school – she could practise this through role-play with other children.
- It might be helpful to talk to parents/carers to clarify where she could have learnt the words and suggest that alternative words are used at home.
- Storm may benefit from a speech and language programme if her general vocabulary is very restricted.
- Storm may need opportunities to express her feelings through role-play, puppets or a visual communication system.

CASE STUDY 21

A child who takes her clothes off

All of a sudden Kayleigh will start to take her clothes off at pre-school. She seems totally oblivious of children and adults when she does this and just stands there.

Possible reasons for this behaviour:

- She likes the sensation of wearing no clothes;
- She feels hot;
- She gets adult attention for doing this;
- Social communication difficulties – not understanding socially acceptable norms;
- She doesn't want to be in the situation.

Strategies:

- Explain to Kayleigh that there are certain times to undress (bedtime, swimming, bathing, PE etc.) – and other times when it is not appropriate. Use a doll to demonstrate, and let her dress and undress the doll.
- Use clothes that are more difficult to remove, e.g. dungarees.
- Suggest she should wear very lightweight clothes.
- Have available a PE kit, shorts and T-shirt for her to change into if she starts to undress.
- Distract Kayleigh as soon as someone notices, and encourage her to do something else.
- Give her lots of praise for looking nice in her clothes.

CASE STUDY 22

A child who spits

Aiden has started to spit a lot at pre-school. He will either spit on his own or will spit at adults or other children.

Possible reasons for this behaviour:

- He is intrigued by the bodily function;
- He recognizes that he gets a response;
- He likes to get noticed;
- He is imitating the behaviour of other people he sees;
- Change of family circumstances;
- A medical reason.

Strategies:

- Explain to Aiden that spitting is not acceptable – if he wants to spit he needs to go into a specified place away from others and spit into a tissue.
- Praise Aiden for playing nicely and reinforce all good behaviours.
- Ask Aiden why he spits.
- Check with parents/carers whether this is happening at home or elsewhere.
- Suggest a check-up with the doctor.

CASE STUDY 23

An over-affectionate child

Lauren often goes straight up to adults, even adults she does not know, and gives them a big hug. She does this constantly and without discrimination. She not only hugs them but will not let go and tries to climb onto their laps if given the opportunity. She also does this to children and has caused some children to complain to an adult.

Possible reasons for this behaviour:

- Lauren needs attention;
- She comes from a very affectionate family;
- She has a limited family or social circle;
- She has the desire to remain younger than her chronological age;
- She doesn't realize that this behaviour is not appropriate in the pre-school setting;
- Lauren has autistic tendencies.

Strategies:

- Explain to Lauren that this is not acceptable behaviour because some people do not like to be hugged all the time – this may need careful explanation because she may be quite vulnerable if she is apt to go to strangers and exhibit this behaviour.
- Give Lauren appropriate levels of attention.
- Give alternatives, e.g. a teddy to cuddle.
- Praise Lauren when she exhibits independent behaviours.

CASE STUDY 24

A child who constantly tells lies

Ben always denies he has done something even if an adult has observed him. Sometimes he makes up stories that at the time seem very plausible. Whenever Ben is seen doing something such as pushing or hitting another child, his first response will be 'I didn't do it' and perhaps even to make something up about one of his peers.

Possible reasons for this behaviour:

- He is attention-seeking;
- There is a lack of consistency in his management;
- Anxiety;
- He may do this as a retreat from the real world.

Strategies:

- Ensure a consistent approach from pre-school staff and, if possible, from parents/carers.
- Make a firm statement of the facts and be accurate: 'I saw you throw the building block and it hit Ashley on the head,' not 'I saw you throw the block at Ashley.'
- Condemn the behaviour, not the child: 'That isn't a nice thing to do,' not 'You are not a nice person/you are a naughty boy.'
- Always give him a way out so that he is not afraid to 'own up': 'I'm sure you didn't mean to hurt Ashley, so say you're sorry and try not to do it again.'
- Don't have any prolonged arguing or explanations from adults.
- Monitor closely – try to divert Ben when he looks as though he is going to lie by providing a true version of events with which he can agree.
- Use stories to model honest behaviour.
- Record serious incidents.

CASE STUDY 25

A child who always has to be 'first'

Charlie always has to be first to start a game. He will push other children out of the way in his rush to be at the front of a line, and becomes difficult if he cannot get his own way.

Possible reasons for this behaviour:

- Charlie likes attention;
- He likes to control adults;
- He has low self-esteem;
- He lacks social awareness;
- Possible social communication disorder.

Strategies:

- Give praise for appropriate behaviour.
- Give Charlie a special job to distract him, e.g. holding the door.
- Place Charlie next to a buddy in the line.
- Change Charlie's place in the line regularly so that he gets used to being in different places. Give the children numbers, then instructions: 'all the ones line up, all the twos' etc. or 'everyone wearing ...'.
- Do the children have to line up? It might be worth considering alternative methods of travelling around the building.

CASE STUDY 26

A child who bites

Jasmine often resorts to biting other children when she cannot get her own way or whenever she feels that things are not going her way. She has even bitten adults in the setting and often refuses to say sorry.

Possible reasons for this behaviour:

- Poor vocabulary – she does not possess the verbal skills to express herself;
- Jasmine may be at an early developmental stage and the biting could just be a reflection of her general development and cognitive abilities – she will need to be treated accordingly. Planning may need adjusting to take her developmental needs into account;
- Inability to control her feelings, especially those of anger;
- Jasmine has learnt that whenever she does this she gets her own way;
- It is an attempt to increase her status and/or power within the family hierarchy;
- Inconsistent management.

Strategies:

- Whenever Jasmine bites, staff should immediately pay attention to the child who has been bitten while initially ignoring Jasmine.
- Jasmine must be told in a very explicit and concise manner that biting will not be tolerated.
- Staff may need to plan very carefully for Jasmine after observing and gathering information about her developmental stage.
- She should have the opportunity to engage with a small group of children regularly in an adult-led activity while appropriate behaviours are modelled.
- Praise should be given whenever Jasmine is able to resolve conflicts without resorting to biting.
- When an incident of biting occurs, staff should always talk to both parents/carers.
- It would be a good idea to implement a management plan for any such incidents and agree this with parents/carers.

CASE STUDY 27

A child demonstrating a fear of people and animals

Peter is a four-year-old boy who has not attended a nursery because of his fear of people other than his mother and grandmother. Peter insists on wearing a baseball cap that he pulls down over his eyes so that he cannot see faces and so that he can avoid eye contact.

When Peter's mother tries to take him out for routine events like shopping or using public transport, he reacts by resisting any attempts to make him board a bus or enter a shop. Peter cries, screams and struggles to such an extent that his mother usually takes him home. Peter's difficulties are impacting significantly upon family life, which to all intents and purposes is confined to the home.

Peter ignores all interactions from people other than his mother and grandmother. When Peter speaks to his mother, his speech is unintelligible and he uses gesture to make his needs and wants clear to her.

Peter likes to stick to the same routines every day and demonstrates inflexibility at home with regard to the food he will eat and the toys he likes to play with. Peter's mother has had to re-home the family dog due to his inability to tolerate being in the same room as the pet.

Possible reasons for this behaviour:

- Peter has a genuine fear of people and animals;
- Peter has discovered he is able to control his life by the use of the above behaviours;
- Peter may have difficulties that could be associated with the Autistic Continuum.

Strategies:

- Peter should be referred to a consultant paediatrician for a developmental assessment.
- Peter's mother should be encouraged and helped to find a suitable nursery/pre-school so that assessments can be made about any possible educational difficulties.
- If possible, the nursery should be assisted with a gentle transition between home and nursery so that Peter is helped to settle into the new environment.

- Peter's mother should consider using visual methods of showing him what will happen – visual time line or timetable of events and including changes to his routine.
- At first, Peter's mother should be encouraged to stay at the nursery and then to leave him for a short time, gradually leaving him for longer so that an hour per day is achieved.
- A visual method of showing routines and other events should be used – pictorial/visual timetable.
- If at all possible, the nursery should provide a key worker who will assist Peter with settling in, providing visual cue cards for points of reference/routines, and with making the transition to using a visual timetable. The visual timetable should always include a picture of home time and Peter's mother collecting him.
- After this, depending upon how successfully Peter accepts the situation, he should be left for a whole session.
- Staff should always use a highly visual method of communicating with Peter and this should include pictures, cue cards and perhaps signing to accompany speech.
- Peter should be encouraged to make choices (from a maximum of two items) and adults should model appropriate language.
- Language models may begin with a single word and then by linking a noun and a verb e.g. 'eat biscuit', 'play car'.
- Peter should be monitored closely to assess the level of his difficulties, with the appropriate outside agencies being involved.
- Peter should be referred to a speech and language therapist.
- Peter should be referred to a dietician.
- Educational agencies should be involved to assess his likely needs upon school entry.

Note:

The above case study is a description of true events with obvious alterations to avoid identification. 'Peter' was successfully integrated into a nursery and now attends for five sessions independently. He was hesitant at first, but demonstrated a real (and surprising) willingness to take part in activities and use toys and equipment, especially the large, well-equipped outdoor play area. At first, Peter kept his baseball cap pulled low down over his eyes. The staff were very willing to help with a very slow and gradual transition and were able to provide an assistant who now supports with 'light touch' and prompting when necessary. Peter uses a visual timetable and is able to make choices using picture cards often accompanied by a single word. Peter has stopped wearing his baseball cap and uses eye contact on his own terms. Peter plays alongside children, tolerating their presence, and responds to adult direction very well. Peter demonstrates good cognitive abilities and is able to count to at least 50, is able to problem-solve, is able to tell the time, and is able to carry out simple functions with numbers. His learning profile is typically uneven for children with his level of difficulty. Peter has been diagnosed with Autistic Spectrum Disorder and is on the waiting list for a place in a special unit for children with ASD.

CASE STUDY 28

A child who eats inappropriate items/objects

Sarah is four years old and has attended the same nursery since she was three.

Sarah eats items such as fluff from the carpet, foam rubber, wool, play dough, uncooked pasta, paint, cake and bread mix, snacks that belong to other children, egg shells, leaves and other assorted items.

Sarah demonstrates this behaviour on a daily basis and appears to ignore all instructions not to do this. Staff at her nursery are concerned that she will eat something that will eventually make her ill.

In all other respects, Sarah's behaviour appears to be age-appropriate.

Possible reasons for this behaviour:

- Sarah has a sensory need that requires assessment;
- Sarah could be suffering from a deficiency in her diet and she is demonstrating an urge to satisfy this;
- Sarah is developmentally delayed.

Strategies:

- Refer Sarah for a sensory assessment.
- The sensory assessment may throw up issues that can be addressed at home and at school.
- Draw up a care plan for Sarah so all staff are aware of the difficulty and how to manage it.
- Refer Sarah to the paediatrician for a medical assessment to rule out possible dietary issues.
- Provide Sarah with a pictorial timetable that includes snack times.
- Provide Sarah with supervision at snack times and make sure that she eats appropriate things at that time.
- Allow Sarah to remove the 'snack picture' and to put it into a 'finished box'.
- Provide Sarah with a visual representation of things she is allowed to eat and things that are not for eating and encourage her to 'sort' into categories.
- Sarah may need a special sensory 'kit' that includes items she can chew safely.

CASE STUDY 29

A child who falls asleep

Daniel is nearly four years old and has attended a pre-school for about 9 months. When he comes into pre-school, he goes straight to the home corner, curls up on an armchair and appears to go to sleep.

When not asleep, Daniel remains either on the chair or on the mat nearby and observes the activity in the pre-school room. He does not interact with other children and only interacts with adults if they ask a direct question, answering with a single word or a nod.

Possible reasons for this behaviour:

- Daniel has an illness that requires investigation;
- Daniel is suffering emotional distress;
- Daniel may be on the Autistic Continuum;
- Daniel is suffering abuse.

Strategies:

- Daniel should be referred to a paediatrician for a full developmental assessment.
- The staff should arrange a meeting with parents to assess whether this behaviour is the norm at home as well as in the pre-school.
- If Daniel has a typical pattern of waking and sleeping at home, efforts should be made to assess whether Daniel finds the environment stressful and resorts to sleep in order to escape from any discomfort.
- Staff should make the physical environment as stress-free as possible.
- Provide a 'retreat' such as a tent or an area that is screened from the general busy areas in the pre-school room.
- Provide Daniel with a pictorial timetable of the session that includes times when he is allowed to use the 'retreat'.
- During other times, structure Daniel's session so that he knows exactly what he will be doing, and equipment and materials he needs for painting etc. should also be included on the timetable.

- Depending upon the outcome of the paediatrician's assessment, staff should monitor any effect the strategies have upon Daniel's ability to remain awake and to improve progress with social interaction.
- If speech, language and social interaction remain limited, staff should use a highly visual method of communicating with Daniel.
- A diary may be useful to record any patterns of sleeping/ waking.

CASE STUDY 30

A child who is oppositional and violent on a constant, daily basis

Donna is a four-year-old girl who has been asked to leave three previous pre-schools for constant defiance and aggression. Donna's behaviour is a cause for concern and she also has some difficulty with speech sound production, thus making her speech slightly difficult to understand.

Donna behaves to her own agenda and refuses to cooperate with even simple instructions to sit and listen to a story or to join a small group of children engaged in a task. Donna responds to unwanted interactions from adults by hitting out at them.

Donna lashes out at other children at random, refuses to share toys and refuses to take turns. Donna likes to have her own way, and bites, hits and scratches other children if they assert themselves.

Staff are at a loss as to how they should tackle Donna, as she behaves to her own agenda from the moment she arrives in the morning and for the duration of the session. Parents of other children are making complaints about bruises and bite marks.

Possible reasons for this behaviour:

- Donna has learned that using aggression is a successful way of getting what she wants;
- Donna has a language disorder;
- Donna has a specific behavioural disorder;
- Donna has never been exposed to boundaries regarding behaviour.

Strategies:

- Steps should be taken to rule out any medical reason for Donna's behaviour.
- An assessment of Donna's speech and language skills should be sought.
- Donna's behaviour should be addressed as a matter of priority.
- A Behaviour Plan should be implemented.
- The plan should highlight behaviours that are not acceptable and the sanctions that will take place as a result.

- The plan should also highlight rewards that will be used for wanted behaviours.
- Avoid using Donna's name when interacting with her over unwanted behaviours, and use her name when staff catch her demonstrating acceptable or wanted behaviours.
- The rewards should be given for wanted behaviours every time at first and could include stickers, praise, time with a favourite toy.
- The Plan should outline how staff will respond to target behaviours so that complete consistency can be maintained.
- Socially unacceptable behaviours like hitting, biting etc should never be ignored and should be dealt with swiftly by implementing sanctions agreed on the Behaviour Plan.
- If 'time out' is to be used as a sanction, this should involve no attention or eye contact from adults. Time out – one minute for every year of the child's life.
- Avoid explanations but stick to the points outlined in the Behaviour Plan, thereby putting the responsibility for the behaviour firmly with Donna.
- The plan should be discussed and agreed with parents so that management can be consistent between home and pre-school.
- A high degree of structure to the session should be imposed upon Donna at first. Choices should be limited at first and then gradually extended in line with Donna's ability to progress.
- A visual timetable of Donna's session should be implemented.
- Donna's session should be shortened at first and if possible, she should be allowed to come into pre-school 15 minutes before all the other children arrive.
- A staff member should go over the timetable with Donna during this time and also go over the Behaviour Plan upon admittance.
- The staff member should supervise Donna closely at first and make sure that she sticks to activities on her visual timetable.
- Gradually, allow Donna a degree of choice regarding activities, but she must stick to these and must complete at least one task directed by an adult.
- Parents should make sure that they arrive at the pre-school at the agreed time and also that they collect Donna when agreed.
- Donna's session should be gradually lengthened depending upon success and the aim should be to integrate her into the full session over time.

- A home/school contact book should be implemented for positive achievements and comments only. This should go back and forth between home and school so that Donna can talk about things she has done well in both settings.
- Give Donna responsibility.
- The general strategy should be viewed as long-term. Behaviours that are entrenched can take a relatively long period to change. Consistency is important.

CASE STUDY 31

A child who has extreme emotional responses to daily events

Ben is a four-year-old child with a stable family background and has attended the same pre-school for nearly two years.

Ben is a very intelligent child with a wide vocabulary and good speech, language and communication skills.

Ben reacts to routine events like being asked to play with a different toy/s by becoming extremely distressed and crying in an almost melodramatic fashion.

Sometimes he walks up and down the room repetitively, mumbling to himself and clutching his head in a despairing manner. Ben's outbursts are out of all proportion to the actual event.

It takes staff a considerable period of time to help Ben regain composure after these episodes.

Ben takes part in activities as long as he thinks he can succeed; if he begins to 'fail' in his opinion, he withdraws. During small group activities/games, Ben only joins in if he can maintain some control over the situation – if not, he withdraws. Ben demonstrates a general lack of awareness of social situations and tends to interact with specific children and adults only.

Ben is inflexible and likes to use props that are carried around with him all day e.g. a small model of Thomas the Tank Engine.

Ben has extreme difficulty understanding the point of view of others. He demonstrates obsessional behaviours and plays with a limited range of things.

Ben is achieving at age-appropriate levels with the EYFSC and is functioning in advance of peers in some areas.

Possible reasons for this behaviour:

- Ben is an intelligent child and has realized that some behaviours result in getting what he wants;
- Ben has issues that could be categorized as 'high functioning' Autistic difficulties;
- Ben has difficulties on the Speech and Language Continuum.

Strategies:

- Staff should gather information about Ben's behaviour and share their concerns with parents in the first instance.

- Ben should be referred to a paediatrician.
- If the outcome of the paediatric assessment results in a diagnosis of ASD the setting should consider implementing some basic managing strategies.
- A behaviour management plan should be implemented so that staff react to outbursts with consistency.
- A personal, visual timetable of the session should be implemented and a high degree of structure should be imposed.
- Ben should be encouraged to stick activities on the timetable and carry these out in order.
- One-to-one working should be included on the timetable.
- During these sessions the following activities can be considered:
    a. identifying emotions from photographs;
    b. asking 'why' questions about pictures of children who are demonstrating emotions;
    c. telling of social stories to encourage thinking about appropriate responses;
    d. sequencing events;
    e. predicting the outcome/ending of a story by using the words 'what CAN happen …';
    f. turn-taking games that have to be completed using a visual method of measuring the time.
- Ben should be encouraged to view his paintings, drawings, models etc with a positive attitude, and adults should praise his efforts and help him to realize that it is quite acceptable if things are not 'perfect'. Examples of children's work could be used in small group situations to highlight positive aspects of the drawings/paintings/models.
- Ben will benefit from help to develop coping structures and strategies that he can rely upon for developing independence.
- Ben may benefit from a notebook that has information about materials and resources he needs for various activities.
- This can be extended to helping with transition from pre-school to school.

AUTISTIC SPECTRUM DISORDER AND SPEECH AND LANGUAGE DISORDER

Children who are attending pre-provisions, nurseries and foundation units and who may or may not have a diagnosis of Autistic Spectrum Disorder (ASD) demonstrate behaviours that are usually described as a 'triad of impairment' in the following areas: speech, language and communication, social interaction and repetitive/stereotypical behaviours. However, as with all children, children with ASD present as unique individuals and in order to manage their difficulties, practitioners will have to 'tailor' strategies to suit rather than using a blanket approach to manage behaviours effectively. In general children with ASD or with speech and language disorders benefit from a highly visual and structured approach to teaching and learning. The following case studies are an attempt to show that although children may have the same diagnosis, strategies should reflect individual needs.

Children with diagnosis of speech and language disorders demonstrate behaviours that can be likened to the behaviours seen in children with an ASD diagnosis. It is the job of an educationalist to identify the primary need and to address this, in partnership with involved professionals and parents, with targeted support. It is important to be consistent, and strategies that work will need to be employed at home and at school for best results.

CASE STUDY 32

Leo, four years old, a child with a diagnosis of ASD

Leo uses complete and grammatically correct sentences to communicate with adults. He has a wide vocabulary and likes to talk to visiting adults as well as staff in his nursery. Leo uses eye contact on his own terms especially when interest levels are high or when he wants something. Leo will sometimes use prolonged eye contact and put his face very close to that of the person he is speaking to. If adults ask Leo a direct question, he is able to supply the correct answer straight away. If he is asked an open-ended question or a 'why' question, Leo will usually ignore this or repeat it. Sometimes, perhaps even an hour later, Leo will 'answer' the question out of context without checking to see whether the relevant adult is nearby. He uses learned jargon or phrases that are not directed to any particular person. Leo is judged to be an able child and is doing very well with the curriculum, being ahead of peers in subjects like mathematical knowledge. However, he becomes very distressed if the routines are changed and if his own notion of what he will be doing during the session is disrupted in any way.

Leo does not interact with peers socially, and prefers to remain on the sidelines of groups although he has recently started to play with one particular child in the setting. Leo puts his hands over his ears frequently during the session.

He likes to play repetitively with a limited range of equipment, usually train tracks or cars.

Leo has no concept of time and will use 'yesterday', 'tomorrow', 'before' and 'after' out of context or inappropriately.

Strategies:

- Implement a high degree of structure to Leo's sessions.
- Implement a visual timetable of Leo's session and break this down into manageable 'chunks'.
- Leo's timetable should preferably run from left to right (rather than top to bottom) and might include arrows to show the direction of 'travel'.
- Always include 'home time'.

- Be very aware that although Leo appears to have good levels of language skills, he may have difficulty understanding more complex language and may require extended time to process this and/or extra visual help to do this. For example, Leo may need a personal copy of the book at story time and an adult to point to key characters/events to aid comprehension.
- Use the vocabulary 'first', 'next', 'last', 'yesterday', 'today', 'tomorrow' to reinforce time concepts along with visual clues on the timetable.
- Provide daily opportunities when Leo arrives for a key worker to discuss the timetable and include any changes to the routine.
- Use frequent verbal/visual reminders about the change.
- Accompany verbal instructions with visual aids or signs whenever possible.
- Provide 'time out' or a refuge for Leo for when he becomes distressed.
- Provide a place of calm in order to balance any distress caused by sensory overload.
- Use targeted support sessions to work on Leo's receptive language skills, e.g. explore whether he understands the use of positional language and also his understanding of complex instructions.
- Use targeted support to explore whether Leo is able to sequence a set of picture cards and whether he can express what is happening.
- Assess whether Leo is able to supply the ending to a familiar repetitive story.
- Assess whether Leo is able to supply the ending to an unfamiliar story.
- Assess Leo's ability to respond to 'why' and 'how' questions and provide opportunities for language modelling.
- Staff may need to consider whether the physical environment can be adapted to accommodate any sensory issues that affect Leo.
- The ongoing input of a speech and language therapist will be useful for planning programmes of work designed to develop Leo's ability to understand and to express language effectively.

CASE STUDY 33

Rachel, four years old, a child with a diagnosis of ASD

Rachel has attended her nursery for over a year and rarely makes eye contact with either adults or children. Rachel uses pointing and gesture in order to indicate need, and sometimes copies a modelled single word. Rachel requires adults to guide her to an activity, without which she would play with the building bricks repetitively by emptying the box they are kept in and then filling it up again. Rachel does not respond to her name being called and does not join in with group activities like singing or doing actions to stories/ rhymes. She pushes other children away if they get too close to her or try to join her in play. Rachel is not toilet trained and shows no awareness of being uncomfortable. Rachel has no sense of danger and an increased pain threshold.

Strategies:

- Rachel has a significant level of need and will require specialist teaching in order to make progress.
- In the nursery, staff should use a highly visual method of communicating with Rachel.
- Staff should use reduced language when addressing Rachel.
- Rachel should be taught to respond to visual cue cards, especially 'stop' for keeping her safe. For example, adults may have to intervene physically if Rachel attempts to do anything that could lead her to hurt herself – this action should be accompanied by a visual sign for 'stop'.
- Other visual aids such as 'good looking', 'good sitting', 'good listening' should be employed regularly.
- Visual cue cards should be made for points of reference and for routine events.
- Rachel should be provided with her own personal cushion for joining group activities.
- Actions to songs etc should be modelled by an adult and Rachel should be assisted to participate via close adult support.
- Rachel should be encouraged to make choices. Adults should offer a maximum of two items and model language for Rachel to copy at first. This should be extended to linking a noun and a verb e.g. 'drink milk' and modelled for Rachel to copy.

- She may require a visual method of making choices depending upon progress by being presented with visual representations of what is on offer, picture cards or photos.
- Rachel should be encouraged to follow simple instruction, e.g. 'get coat' accompanied by a visual aid. Adults should stick to using key words and only give one instruction at a time.
- She may benefit from being taught signing.
- Rachel will benefit from the use of photographs of herself in the nursery carrying out routine events.
- She will require adults to model play and to use language modelling to accompany this.
- Rachel will require the ongoing input of a speech and language therapist for programmes of work to develop her ability to communicate.
- Rachel may benefit from a sensory assessment.

CASE STUDY 34

Liam, four years old, a child with a diagnosis of ASD

Liam has attended nursery for over a year. He has always been viewed by staff as a very emotional child with exaggerated responses to daily events. Staff have no concerns about Liam's ability to understand even complex ideas and instructions, and describe his use of language as 'excellent'. He uses well-constructed sentences, is able to hold conversations with adults and to describe stories, outings and to predict outcomes with age-appropriate language skills. Liam's progress with the Early Years Foundation Stage Curriculum is age-appropriate or even in advance of peers.

Liam responds with extreme emotion, throwing himself on the floor, wailing and sobbing if not allowed to play with his favourite toy. He has an obsessional interest in trains, Thomas the Tank Engine in particular. He holds a model train at all times, taking it everywhere with him. Liam is extremely inflexible, demanding that the same route is followed home, to nursery, to the shops and that the same routines are adhered to in the home. Liam appears to be unable to recognize when people are sad, happy or angry. He appears unable to accept that drawings/paintings that he considers 'wrong' are quite acceptable and are valued by staff and parents. If he thinks that he has done something incorrectly, he will respond with heightened emotion, crying and flinging himself onto the floor. When asked to join in with small group games, Liam often plays for a short time before withdrawing if he cannot control the outcome. Liam's mother reports that he is often rude to strangers in the street or shops without warning. He uses echolalia and demonstrates word finding difficulties on an inconsistent basis. When he cannot think of the exact word he wants, Liam becomes emotionally distressed. Staff and parents are concerned about how Liam will cope with transferring to school.

Strategies:

- Liam may benefit from a full language assessment from a speech and language therapist even though he appears to have good verbal skills.
- The assessment may indicate possible processing difficulties.

- Liam will benefit from a visual timetable of daily events. Changes to the routine should be included and he should be given frequent verbal reminders about the change.
- A structure to 'unstructured' times of the day like 'tidy up' or transition times of the day should be planned for Liam to rely upon, for example he will need photos of himself lining up or tidying up.
- Liam should be introduced to a personal method of coping with perceived 'failure'. For example, he should be shown different outcomes to painting or drawing and encouraged to describe how 'good' they are.
- Liam should be exposed to photographs of faces showing a range of emotions, and assessments should be made about whether he is able to identify these.
- Social stories could be used in order to highlight the difference between trivial and significant events and the way in which people respond to these.
- Social skills groups could be used to reinforce appropriate social responses to a range of situations.
- Liam would benefit from regular small group activities to practise turn-taking and cooperative social interaction skills.
- Staff may need to consider whether the physical environment is suitable from a sensory point of view.
- Liam may benefit from 'time out' or a refuge to help him to calm down when distress levels are high.
- He will benefit from an extended 'transition' period to school. Staff will need to make contact with the receiving school and plan a more intensive transition package into school. Liam will require a visual representation of school transition on his timetable. More visits than usual should be planned to the receiving school. At home, Liam should be encouraged to put his school uniform on and take the route to his new school well before the beginning of the term. He should practise putting his P.E. kit on and getting dressed again so that he is independent. He may require a sequential picture reminder of how to do this.
- Strategies to help Liam to cope with moderating his emotional responses should involve making him dependent upon a set of personal coping mechanisms rather than being dependent upon key workers and other adults. Liam will encounter many adults during his school career and unfortunately this could result in inconsistencies in management.

- In future, consideration will have to be given to strategies that help Liam with collecting the right materials and resources for different subject lessons. A personal notebook with timetables, equipment needed for lessons etc. will help to reduce stress levels.
- Liam may benefit from a 'transition' area that he can access to check his timetable, check what equipment is needed and perhaps a 'workstation' that is set up with a structure and a format for beginning and completing a task. The workstation may be a booth or a screened area depending upon need.
- Emphasis should be placed upon providing an educational environment that is planned and organized to reduce possible raising of stress levels.

CASE STUDY 35

Jake

Jake was the first baby in the family and was given constant attention by various family members for his first two years. Jake's mum then went back to work and Jake attended the local day nursery. There had been a gradual part-time introduction to nursery staff and routine and Jake's mum ensured he seemed happy at nursery before returning to work. Jake had an allocated caseworker whom he looked forward to seeing each morning.

Jake appeared to settle for the first week but then kept asking people 'When go home?' and they kept telling him it was time for play and lunch and afternoon rest first. He did not appear to be satisfied with this and kept repeating the question and becoming more agitated, waiting as near to the door as he could.

Possible reasons for this behaviour:

- Jake does not yet understand the concept of time;
- Jake does not understand the language and words said to him;
- Jake may find something disturbing at the nursery.

Strategies:

- Maintain close observation to try to determine whether there are specific times or conditions that are upsetting Jake. He may be getting overtired and may need an extra nap.
- It may be helpful to have a picture board of the pattern of the day. Jake can take down the cards as the activities are complete. This will give Jake a clear idea of the pattern to the day and he should be able to look at the board so that a routine is established. Photographs could be useful.
- Use very clear vocabulary so that Jake associates the words with the pictures or photographs so that he will gradually become less reliant on the daily planner.

CASE STUDY 36

Rosie

Rosie started pre-school at two and a half years. Her mum told the pre-school that she was 'quite hard work' at home and had started to become more difficult.

Pre-school staff soon noticed that Rosie would sneakily take other children's toys and if they were taken away from her either by staff or by another child she would lie on the floor and kick and scream. She would keep this up for about half an hour and would kick any person who came near her. This was mentioned to Rosie's mum who said that this was not typical of Rosie's behaviour at home, although she did scream if she didn't get what she wanted. Rosie's mum said she did not always give in to her.

Possible reasons for this behaviour:

- Rosie is getting mixed messages from her mother's response to her behaviour;
- Rosie is finding it more difficult to share with other children;
- Rosie feels she may eventually get what she wants at nursery if she screams long enough, as this is the way it often works at home. Rosie's behaviour is becoming more and more exaggerated as this has not currently worked for her.

Strategies:

- The only way to make it clear to Rosie that this behaviour will not be tolerated is to consistently maintain the rule that snatching is not allowed. This may take several weeks. It will be important to ensure that Rosie will not hurt herself and to move the other children away from her until she has calmed down. If possible, Rosie should be encouraged to go into a specific 'calming corner' on her own where she has specific toys to play with or cloth books that she cannot tear up. If possible play some soothing music in that area to enable her to calm down.
- Rosie could be encouraged or taught to play with toys with other children, one child to begin with and an adult present.

- It may be useful to discuss Rosie's behaviour with her mother so that she is clear about the consistent rules in the pre-school. Rosie's mother should be encouraged to also be clear and consistent about boundaries if possible. There could be a contact book between home and pre-school where Rosie gets a star or special sticker for every time she follows the rules set.

CASE STUDY 37

Frankie

Frankie had been at pre-school since she was a baby and appeared to have settled in well. When she was nearly two years old she started to bite the other children at pre-school, including the very young children who were just crawling. Children became very frightened of being near her. She even bit the adults who tried to come near her to stop her. Scolding or moving her away from the situation did not deter her at the next opportunity she got. Staff became very anxious.

Possible reasons for this behaviour:

- Frankie saw that she got a reaction whenever she bit anyone. It is possible that the focus was on younger children in the pre-school and less on her so she started to demand attention in the most effective way she was able at the time;
- Frankie may find biting an effective way of getting what she wants at home;
- Frankie may use biting as a way of showing her frustration.

Strategies:

- A very effective way of helping Frankie is to buy a special wrist band that can be chewed. Frankie should be encouraged to use the wrist band whenever she shows signs of attempting to bite others.
- Frankie could be given her own special toys to bite when she wants to bite someone.
- This should be discussed with Frankie's parents/carers and they could be asked to record when the biting happens at home. This should also happen at pre-school, and a behavioural support plan could be devised.
- Frankie may have additional difficulties so it would be advisable to keep a record of her behaviour, observe which toys she chooses to play with, and seek further support if this continues.

CASE STUDY 38

JT

JT came into pre-school like a tornado. He was about two years old and immediately knocked anything he could off the shelving, threw all the books out of the bookcase and started to try to pull toys apart. He seemed oblivious of others and did not notice their disapproving looks or even when staff told him not to do that. His mother was in such a position that she needed to work and just left him each morning, coming back each evening to a catalogue of problems.

Possible reasons for this behaviour:

- JT is totally fascinated by seeing how things work and likes to see what happens when he knocks this over etc;
- JT may have ADHD (Attention Deficit Hyperactivity Disorder) or autism, although these disorders are truly difficult to diagnose until the child is much older;
- Boys are generally more physical in their play, which needs to be appropriately channelled;
- JT engages in this behaviour at home and has no boundaries set;
- JT has language and understanding difficulties.

Strategies:

- JT should be shown how to behave for specific parts of the day, e.g. a picture timetable for when he comes into the pre-school.
- A specific caseworker allocated to JT should collect him from outside the pre-school and spend individual time with him.
- Calm music could be played as a background in the pre-school. Research has shown that soft background music can reduce noise level and unwanted behaviour.
- Ensure JT's mother is clear about how he is expected to behave in pre-school and to encourage her to reward JT for good behaviour at home. Rewards should also be given at pre-school.
- JT may need to be given a more physical activity as soon as he enters pre-school such as a sit on toy he can drive around. A clear physical programme may need to be designed for him.

Settling Children into Pre-school to Diminish Behavioural Problems

Starting pre-school can be a very emotional time for both parents and the children. Most children settle well but there can often be teething problems. With babies and younger children there is often a situation of separation anxiety. Most babies will go through a normal phase in their development at about 9 months when they become more aware of people around them and feel more comfortable with their main carer/carers. In these cases it will be important that the baby or toddler becomes fully acquainted with the pre-school staff and environment and, ideally, has one main carer. This can take careful planning and time.

There are now many situations where the main carer needs to continue working within a year of the birth of the baby and provision needs to be made for the child's emotional as well as physical care. Some tips are:

- Spend a few weeks getting the child used to his new environment, gradually leaving him for longer periods.
- Take in some of the child's special toys or a special blanket.
- Ensure staff are clear about the child's likes and dislikes.
- Younger babies will often benefit by an article of clothing the carer has worn being left when baby needs to sleep, as young children respond to smell.
- It is important that the carer feels as comfortable as possible when leaving the child in pre-school as children soon pick up on a carer's anxiety. However concerned you are (and almost all carers are), give the child the impression that he will be happy and secure.
- It will be essential that appropriate provision is made for children with disabilities.
- Carers should be able to contact the pre-school by phone or e-mail to check on their child's welfare.

Settling Children into Pre-school

For some children, this may be their first experience of being with other children and needing to share. Almost all children starting pre-school will not yet have managed to represent their feelings in a socially acceptable way, and staff will need to try to interpret what message the child is attempting to give through his behaviour. Some children will still have difficulties with language, and others may have disabilities that have not been apparent in the home setting, such as autistic spectrum characteristics or ADHD.

Basic difficulties could be:

- temper tantrums where the child has not yet managed to learn a more socially acceptable way of showing their confusion;
- fussiness where children will insist on doing things they way they were done at home (such as Mum tidying everything away) or listening to a story sitting on a knee;

- the ultra-quiet child who stands out by not joining in with activities or does not like noise;
- children finding their situation overpowering and constantly wanting to go home;
- home situations impinging on how the child responds to adults and other children;
- children with special needs of various sorts;
- children who continue to cling to parents or have separation anxiety.

Supporting Children with Special Educational Needs

There needs to be special awareness of both the needs of children and their parents during the transition phases of children first starting pre-school or school. It is often devastating for parents to be told that their child will have special learning needs when a baby is born or very young, and they grieve for the 'normal' child they always wished for. Many parents will remain optimistic and hope that their child may eventually 'pick up' as they develop, and hope that their child may manage a mainstream pre-school and school where they will have local friends. It can be totally devastating again when parents begin to realize that their child is not coping in the way they had hoped.

Suggestions for Transition Phase Staff

- Reassure parents that you understand that it is more difficult to leave children with disabilities and that that is normal and to be expected.
- Inform parents that special support will be provided as necessary.
- If there are highly significant concerns, staff should ask parents whether they feel greater support would be useful or whether an informal assessment within the pre-school/school setting would be useful.
- Never suggest any diagnosis. Leave that to the medical profession.

Some ideas that might help parents in preparing their children:
- Talk to the child about how exciting things will be.
- Try to take the child to see the pre-school and become accustomed to its layout, such as toilets and outdoor area.
- Try to involve another family who may be starting at the same time so the child has a friend.
- Once the child is relatively settled when you are there, tell the child you will be back later and give him a kiss and then leave promptly without continuously looking back. Make this a regular pattern.

What is important for maintaining a good pre-school?
- At pre-school, placing children in appropriate age settings with staff who are qualified to work with that age group.

- Ensure staff training is regular and constantly updated.
- Clear rules should be given to all staff, and all staff should have the same approach to behaviour problems.
- Parents should be notified and involved as soon as behavioural difficulties become noticeable. Early intervention is the key to success.
- There need to be clear boundaries, and parents should be aware of pre-school boundaries and encouraged to support their young children at home.
- Remember that young children soon recognize that different rules and boundaries exist in different environments and respond to these. A child's difficult behaviour at home may not be exhibited in a pre-school where the rules and boundaries are clear.

The Ways Young Boys Learn

Many boys develop developmentally differently to girls, as most pre-school workers will no doubt notice! They tend to need a more physically-based curriculum and generally are far more boisterous than girls. These boys enjoy play-fighting and they tend to learn far more through physical and practical experiences in the early stages.

Ways to help

- Allow boys more opportunities for physical and practical outdoor play where possible. Allow girls a similar opportunity which they may also want.
- Ask the boys what games they like, and try to accommodate them. For example, they may want knights and dragons so a theme would be built around that where the girls can also join in. Making up stories, making costumes, doing some drama could evolve from this. It is likely that there will be stories based on themes that interest the children so they will also learn to sit quietly and listen for short periods.
- Offer various building equipment and let the boys make whatever they want initially and play outside with it if possible. The aim is to provide as much outdoor play as possible for young children with space to run around.
- Young children, especially boys, love digging. If possible a section of a garden area could be set aside for digging and growing fast-growing vegetables.
- Boys will learn far more readily if they are interested and motivated and allowed to be creative in their building and play.
- By allowing boys to become more involved in physical, practical play they will become more confident and creative as they approach a more formal education in future years.
- Most boys are likely to have shorter concentration spans and so need a varying programme during each session. A typical way of supporting boys could be to say 'When you have finished your colouring then you can play with the bikes outside' so that boys gradually develop skills of concentration and completing activities.

Managing the environment (including the role of the Teaching Assistant)

The space

Display and learning resources

Managing staff

Communicating

General good practice strategies

Strategies for Children with Behavioural Difficulties

Practitioners can do a lot to create a space and climate that fosters good behaviour in every sense. The features of the physical environment, such as the size and layout, colours and lighting, and temperature of an area can have an effect upon everyone's mood and the way in which children behave. For example, a large, cold, echoing hall encourages children of all ages to run around: it offers an invitation for children and adults to raise their voices and is not conducive to settling down to any type of learning activity. By using screens and furniture to divide the space available into specific areas such as a book area, quiet drawing area, home corner, large play and sand/water tray areas, you can create a more secure and comfortable environment. The use of soft furnishings such as mats, cushions, curtains and wall displays will help to absorb sound in an otherwise noisy hall as well as making it more cosy and inviting.

The space

- If the hall/room is very large, think about creating different areas for different activities. Use screens, curtains, furniture, plants and shelving to divide a large space into more cosy areas where children feel secure.
- Try to provide some quiet areas that are sectioned off from the more noisy activities to encourage appropriate behaviours for various activities and reduce distraction for the child who is sharing a book, concentrating on a matching activity or listening to a tape. Identify a 'time out' spot.
- Make sure children can move freely between furniture/displays at appropriate speeds and without invading the personal space of others.
- Provide adequate storage for coats and other belongings and ensure that the children know where this is – some children panic if they don't know where their things are. A supply of clothes pegs to keep hats, coats and gloves together may be one way of preventing lost property problems. Simple shoe bags are also useful to keep not only both shoes but also other small items of clothing together. Ask parents/carers to make these, or enlist the help of someone with a sewing machine to make a 'job lot' for the group (curtains/ bed linen from charity shops will provide cheap material). Getting children used to looking after their belongings will be valuable training for 'big school'.

- Label everything with words and pictures.
- Make sure that storage is at child height and that

everyday equipment such as pencils, paper and crayons is accessible so that the children can organize their own equipment.

- Think carefully about ventilation. Is enough fresh air available? Can windows be opened safely on a hot day?
- Lighting can have a big effect on mood and concentration. Natural light is best, but where artificial lighting is needed, try to ensure that this is as 'natural' as possible and adequate for the tasks undertaken. Good lighting will be especially important for children with visual impairment.
- Temperature is an important factor in feeling comfortable (and amenable!) – even adults are more likely to be irritable and tetchy if they are hot and bothered, thirsty and lethargic. Try to maintain an even temperature in the setting and help parents/carers to provide suitable clothing by suggesting a layered style of dress – T-shirt under sweater or sweatshirt, under coat – to allow children to peel off when they get hot. Keep a box of spare clothing – parents/carers are usually happy to donate outgrown items. In cold weather, encourage warm clothing and build in regular exercise/movement activities rather than relying on high-setting heating.
- Security is important; ensure that children can't leave the room/building on their own – is it possible to fit high door handles?
- Display general information (holiday dates etc.) on a noticeboard but back up with verbal reminders – not all adults can or do read notices.

Display and learning resources

- There should be a visual timetable of the day positioned at child height – use pictures and/or photographs and arrows to show sequence. Involve the children in the discussion about the structure of the day by asking them to find the appropriate picture of activities to put up on the board. A visual or pictorial timetable can be a simple set of photos or pictures of the activities of the day. These could be laminated and stuck to a child-height board (by using Velcro® on the back) or hung on a line every morning with the help of the children. This visual reminder of the session helps to give structure to the child with difficulties and is good for all children. When changes to the routine are planned this will help to warn children in a very clear way about what will happen.

- A box of visual aids should be kept ready for instruction times to accompany talk/discussions.
- Have clearly visible rules on display with accompanying pictures.

- Display the children's work as professionally as you can, thereby placing instant value on their efforts.
- Choose easy-to-put-on aprons so that children are encouraged to get themselves ready for painting/water play activities.

Managing staff

Having created an early years setting that has all the physical features of a calm, comfortable and welcoming learning environment, how do you keep it that way?

How practitioners work together and manage the children in their care strongly affects the way in which those children feel and behave. For example, if it is the usual policy for adults to talk to each other using raised voices, or to shout across to the person on the other side of the room, it is hardly surprising if the children do the same. Providing good role models in the way you behave and the way in which you talk to both adults and children are vital parts of your management strategy.

The role of the teaching assistant

The role of the teaching assistant is becoming increasingly complex. Depending upon how schools manage their inclusion systems, it can be that teaching assistants are more and more involved in the support of children with additional needs.

Key areas for the teaching assistant:

- preparing materials for activities and tasks;
- helping children to participate;
- helping children to be independent;
- supporting individual children;
- supporting the teacher;
- supporting the curriculum;
- supporting the school;
- working with outside agencies;
- assisting with physical needs;
- modelling good practice;
- freeing up the teacher to teach smaller groups;
- providing feedback;
- helping to raise standards;
- identifying early signs of disruptive behaviours.

Inclusion managers give much consideration to the training needs of staff, and many teaching assistants have become experienced at identifying needs and assisting with meeting these.

Behaviour difficulties are associated with a range of additional or special educational needs. In the very young child, perhaps attending a large foundation unit, consideration will need to be given to the physical environment, to groupings, to strategies for meeting needs. Behaviour difficulties arise out of complex situations, and careful consideration will need to be applied to the identification of special needs and to meeting these.

Large foundation units with perhaps over 100 children may represent a difficult environment for a child with behaviour difficulties. Awareness about the types of behaviour being demonstrated and recording these in observations are important for future planning. Teaching assistants should be trained in observing in a range of contexts and in objective recording.

Visual representations of basic rules, visual timetables and clear visual aids for key points of reference should be clearly displayed for the whole group. Teaching assistants will need to identify those children with additional needs in whole-group situations so that individual support can be offered in terms of assisting attention and listening, and reinforcing language. Children with difficulties should be seated towards the front of the group and to one side.

For instructions given to the whole group a similar approach may be required in addition to behaviour modelling. For example, when a set of instructions is issued, the teaching assistant may break these down into simple, clear instructions, one at a time and accompanied with modelling or visual aid if necessary.

For unstructured times of the day, e.g. transition from one place to another, tidy up or snack, there will need to be extra support in terms of a 'structure' that can be relied upon for most situations. For play times or outdoor sessions, some children will require a personal plan and perhaps a buddy system, place of refuge, set activities or the opportunity to withdraw.

Teaching assistants should give due consideration to the language they use to address children with behaviour and or language-processing difficulties. In general, reduced language – key words – should be used, especially when trying to get a child to comply or when giving instructions. Lengthy explanations should be avoided.

Unacceptable behaviours should not be ignored but should be dealt with swiftly in accordance with the behaviour policy of the school. Behaviours that are not causing harm to others, e.g. going under the table, refusing to take a hat off etc., should probably be ignored since to highlight these can result in even greater 'offending'. Obsessive behaviours should be ignored if they are not having a significant impact upon the child's ability to take part in activities or to make progress. Some children can be quite easily distracted from repetitive actions and can be encouraged to take part in a task or activity. If behaviours such as repetition or obsession take over a child's time completely, discussions should take place about how to address these. The involvement of other professionals may be sought in the first instance in order to establish what the causes are.

For children with significant behaviour difficulties, teaching assistants may be required to record behaviour. Any recording should be factual, objective and should include the antecedent, the behaviour and the consequence.

(See *Tried and Tested, Play and Learning in the Early Years* for examples of observation and recording sheets). These can be easily adapted to the developmental level of the child.

Communicating

- Use a calm, clear, unhurried voice.
- Be assertive and 'tell' children what you would like them to do – a legitimate response to a question such as 'Would you like to sit here?' is 'No.' It is better to say 'I would like you to sit on the carpet.'
- Do not talk about children or their families while they can overhear you unless it is to praise them. If possible, provide somewhere discreet for parents/carers to talk to you in private.
- Before every session make expectations about behaviour very clear (use positive language, e.g. 'speak quietly').
- Use simple instructions, one or two at a time, e.g. 'Hang your coat up' rather than 'Hang your coat up, take your name card, put it in the box and then sit on the carpet.' When the child has completed one task, then give the next instruction.
- Do not assume that all children have understood what to do. Some are very adept at disguising the fact that they do not understand every word spoken. Check understanding – 'Darren, can you remember two things I said about playing in the water? … Who can help him out?'
- Make children aware of the consequences of breaking the rules: 'I hope everyone will sit still and listen to the story. If anyone starts shouting out or moving around, they will be spoiling the story for everyone else. Mrs Hopkins will take them to the time out corner and they won't find out what happens to Harry in the story.'

General good practice strategies

- Give one member of your staff the responsibility of meeting and greeting every child and adult each day on a rota system. This can help to create good working relationships with parents/carers and provide an opportunity for passing on information.
- During adult–adult interaction, model appropriate behaviours such as being polite, patient, understanding etc.
- Always model the expected behaviours, for example saying 'thank you' when given a drink or biscuit or asking a child, 'May I share that toy with you?'
- Let off steam only when the children are gone – unless you can provide a good model for managing stress! 'Oh dear! This stapler keeps going wrong

and I'm getting into a temper with it. I'm going to put it down now and try it again later.'

- Appoint a trusted adult for a particular child to go to for support when he is feeling anxious or angry.
- Use group/circle times to discuss any issues relating to behaviour in an anonymous manner. Use characters in stories or puppets. Always bear in mind that some children do not like speaking in front of groups of people – that preference ought to be respected.
- Use a device such as a rain stick to gain attention without having to raise your voice – a child could be responsible for shaking this when you give a sign.
- Have a puppet which goes into 'hiding' if it gets too noisy.
- Have rewards ready for appropriate behaviours and give them out instantly.
- Ignore any inappropriate behaviours (health and safety permitting) and praise the other children who are behaving well.
- Employ a buddy system if children are old or mature enough to gain from this role modelling. This is where a mature, well-behaved child is paired up with a child who will benefit from his positive influence.
- Use a home–school contact book that contains positive comments so that parents/carers and pre-school staff can highlight the 'good' rather than dwell on the negative.
- Try not to use story time as a 'tidy up' time for other staff or as a time for putting up displays. This provides an alternative focus of attention for the children.
- Structure the day so that children are not expected to sit for long periods on hard flooring (try this yourself – it doesn't take long to become uncomfortable on some surfaces).
- Be prepared to abandon some activities if they are causing unexpected results – even (or especially) if an Ofsted inspector is present!
- Make sure activities are appropriate and that interest levels are high. For example, make sure that activities provide direct experiences: 'doing' helps the learning process. Ensure that children can identify with topics by relating them to their own experiences so that they are more meaningful. This will maximize curiosity levels and hopefully minimize off-task behaviours.
- Anticipate behaviours – intervene quickly at the early stages of problematic behaviours.
- Recognize achievements and make positive comments, e.g. 'You must be really pleased with that painting, I see that you have really tried hard to use all the colours on the table.'
- Remove items causing inappropriate behaviours.

Strategies for Children with Behavioural Difficulties

Visual timetable of the session

This will need to be broken down into manageable 'chunks' depending upon the age and development of the child.

A visual timetable can be used at home as well as in an educational setting. Some children may require sequential pictures of everyday events, for example the sequence of dressing, washing, brushing teeth, bathing etc. Simple line drawings are best. For easy use, a laminated base with Velcro® squares is advisable. Pictures of events can easily be stuck onto the base and changed when necessary. The child should be involved in placing the pictures. Changes to the timetable should be included and frequent verbal reminders about the change should be employed.

Visual aids

Children with behaviour difficulties benefit from a high degree of visual aid to accompany speech. The aids should be as simple as possible – simple black line drawings on white card work well. Sequential pictures for everyday events and routines are useful.

Choice making

Children with difficulties require simple choices at first. Adults should offer a maximum of two things to choose from and gradually extend these according to the developmental level of the child.

Behaviour plan

Settings should draw up behaviour plans for children with behaviour difficulties. This should be drawn up with parental consent and input. The plan should highlight how staff will respond to behaviours so that consistency can be maintained; for example how staff will handle aggression, swearing, running away etc. Sanctions and rewards should be outlined. The plan can be carried over into the home for consistency, but ALL family members would need to stick to it to have maximum impact.

Visual rules

All settings should have a set of visual rules on display. They need to be very simple and easily remembered. Individual children should be reminded upon entry to the setting what the rules are, and should be encouraged to see themselves as responsible for their own behaviour. If the rules are broken, staff should avoid lengthy explanations and stick to the points on the behaviour plan/visual rules.

Good sitting, good looking, good listening

Settings should consider visual methods of reminding children of expected or wanted behaviours, and simple visual cue cards are a successful way of achieving this.

Stop sign

A universal 'stop' sign can be very useful for children who have difficulty responding to 'No.'

Stop, look and listen

A visual sign for gaining attention is useful when children are engaging in disruptive behaviour or are becoming excitable.

Time out

If possible, time out should only be used for short periods (as a general rule, one minute for every year of the child's age). The place in which time out is used should be free of stimuli; adults should give no attention either negative or positive, and no eye contact.

Sanctuary

A place of sanctuary may be beneficial. This could be a screened area, a tent or den or simply a bean bag.

Home/school liaison books

A book that goes back and forth between home and school is useful for raising self-esteem. The book should contain positive comments only and possibly things/activities/achievements that can be shared.

Responsibility

Give children responsibility. For example, depending upon the age and developmental level of children, they can be 'helper' for the day, be responsible for tidying up, run errands for adults, be responsible for an area of the nursery/school, help at snack times. Responsibility raises self-esteem.

Exit cards

Depending upon routines and staffing, exit cards are a way of giving children the choice of going into another room or place in the setting via the use of a known system.

Rewards

Reward wanted behaviours every time at first. Reward realistically; for example use praise, tokens, time with a favourite activity or toy.

Use of names

Use a child's name when highlighting wanted behaviours. Try to avoid using their name when noticing negative behaviours.

The Code of Practice and its implications for pre-school settings

Summary

Behaviour can change programme

Working in partnership with parents

What do we mean by 'parental responsibility'?

Transition to school

The Code of Practice for special educational needs (SEN) is a document issued by the Department for Education and Skills (DfES). It gives guidance to practitioners on how to identify and provide for a range of special needs, including those related to behavioural, emotional and social development.

Since 2002, all early years settings must have regard to the Code of Practice. This means that they must appoint a special educational needs co-ordinator (SENCO), a practitioner with some special training to whom they can refer for advice and guidance. In addition there is an area SENCO who covers several settings. Early years settings must also have a special educational needs policy that sets out a system for identifying children with special or 'additional' needs and supporting them within the setting. Criteria for this are set out in the 'principles and policies' chapter of the Code of Practice and detailed in paragraphs 1:23 to 1:38. It is worth considering having a written behaviour policy as part of this so that staff and parents/carers are in no doubt about your rules and expectations. It also removes any uncertainties about how staff should respond to different behaviours in the setting.

The Code of Practice sets out the following model of intervention:

- **Early Years Action** is triggered by the practitioner or the parent/carer of a child who is presenting persistent emotional and/or behavioural difficulties that are significant enough to be impacting upon the child's learning and/or upon the learning of the other children. Staff in the setting need to gather information in the form of observations, assessments and information from parents (there is an example of a recording pack in Appendix 1). After consultation with the SENCO, they should then consider drawing up an individual education plan (IEP). The IEP outlines short-term targets set for the child, the teaching strategies and the provision to be put in place, when the plan is to be reviewed, and the outcome of the action taken. Early Years Action is characterized by the setting being able to meet the needs of a child with SEN without the support/advice of outside agencies. There are examples of plans on pp. 108–109. In general, the priority behaviour should be targeted first in small, achievable steps. The targets should be SMART:
  - Specific
  - Measurable
  - Achievable
  - Relevant
  - Timed.
- **Early Years Action Plus** is characterized by the ongoing input of outside agencies such as an educational psychologist or a speech and language therapist. The appropriate specialists will have input to the child's IEP, outlining a small number of specific targets (two or three) and details of how these will be met. Everyone concerned with the child should attend regular review meetings and progress should be carefully monitored.

- **Statutory assessment** is used for a small minority of children with very significant needs. Parents/carers or practitioners can ask the local education authority (LEA) to make an assessment of the child's needs. The LEA will then decide whether or not to write a statement of special educational needs that sets out the provision that must be made for the child. This is a legally binding document. As part of an LEA assessment, the early years setting will be asked for information on the child, whether outside agencies were consulted and what strategies have been put in place.

Summary

When there is concern about a child:

- observe the child and record specific instances of worrying behaviour;
- be explicit about the difficulties as you see them;
- talk to his parents/carers;
- discuss the child with all staff and draw up a behaviour management plan/ strategy to tackle the problem;
- monitor the effectiveness of this strategy;
- if there is no/very little progress, consider drawing up an IEP with specific targets, timescale and success criteria (how you will know that a target has been reached);
- intervention should be at Early Years Action if staff in the setting feel they can meet the child's needs;
- intervention should be at Early Years Action Plus if there is ongoing outside agency input.

Behaviour can change programme

A behaviour management plan is a working strategy that is devised in partnership with parents/carers. This plan describes strategies that will be employed by all staff working with the child. It may also outline some aims for the parents/carers and the child himself on which to work. The plan/programme is regularly evaluated and updated and provides evidence that a number of strategies have been planned and implemented before seeking further advice. Remember, some children need longer 'settling in' periods, and differentiating like this may meet the child's needs without necessarily taking the SEN route. There is an example format of a behaviour management programme below.

Behaviour Can Change Programme

Name of child

_____

List of strengths

_____

List of difficulties

_____

Priority difficulty

_____

Desired outcome

_____

Strategy to be used

_____

How will the child be rewarded

_____

What to do if behaviour occurs

_____

How will the behaviour be recorded

_____

Date Started _____   Signed _____

Date of Review _____

Working in partnership with parents

The Code of Practice highlights the importance of professionals working in partnership with parents. This is important in enabling children to achieve their potential.

Parents:

- have a critical role to play in their children's education;
- have detailed knowledge of their child's progress through developmental stages;
- have important information about early health and developmental checks and will be able to provide details of contacts with other professionals, e.g. speech and language therapists, physiotherapists etc.;
- have problems and difficulties of their own – be understanding and realistic in your expectations;
- may lack confidence in playing out their role – give them encouragement and practical support.

What do we mean by 'parental responsibility'?

It is important that professionals understand who has parental responsibility for a child. The Children Act 1989 uses the phrase 'parental responsibility' to sum up the collection of duties, rights and authority that a parent has in respect of a child. In the event of family breakdown, both married parents will retain parental responsibility even if they then live in different households. In relation to unmarried parents, only the mother will have parental responsibility unless the father has been granted parental responsibility by the court or a parental agreement has been reached with the mother. Where a residence order is in place in respect of a non-parent (e.g. grandparent), that person will have parental responsibility for the duration of the order.

If a child is 'looked after' by a local authority, he may either be on a care order or be voluntarily accommodated.

First point of contact

The pre-school is often the parents' first point of contact with the education system. Remember that you are laying the foundations for effective partnership for the next 16 years or so. A negative experience with staff in the pre-school setting can sour a parent's attitude to 'teachers' for the rest of the child's school life – especially if the parent had a less than enjoyable time at school.

When there is concern about a child's behaviour, parents should be fully involved in the pre-school-based response for their child. The purpose of any intervention or programme of action should be explained carefully to them and they should be told about the local parent partnership service.

- Pre-schools must tell parents when they first identify that a child has SEN.
- Pre-schools should keep records of their discussions with parents from when they first identify that a child has SEN. These records should be brief, recording key information given and parents' opinions in a standard format (an example can be found in Appendix 1).

Communication

To make communication with parents and carers effective, pre-schools should:

- acknowledge and draw on parental knowledge and expertise in relation to their child;
- recognize the personal and emotional investment of parents and be aware of their feelings – focus on the child's strengths as well as areas of additional need;
- ensure that parents understand procedures, are aware of how to access support in preparing their contributions, and are given documents to be discussed well before meetings;
- respect the different views people may hold about an issue and seek ways to ensure all views are heard and recorded;
- respect the differing needs of parents themselves, such as a disability or communication and linguistic barriers;
- recognize the need for flexibility in the timing and structure of meetings;
- provide a comfortable and welcoming area for meetings;
- encourage parents to 'bring a friend' to meetings if they would find this helpful;
- make sure the meeting has an agenda and a realistic time limit;
- keep meetings friendly but business-like;
- be prepared to make home visits;
- define routes of referral to other sources of information and support;
- make sure written reports are as jargon-free as possible;
- ensure that parents are aware of an IEP, understand the targets and that everyone is working consistently to support the child.

Pre-schools working in partnership with parents

- It is vital that pre-schools welcome and encourage parents to participate from the outset and throughout their child's time at the pre-school.
- Pre-schools need to regularly review their policies to ensure they encourage active partnership with parents and do not present barriers to participation.
- Pre-schools should seek to actively work with their local parent partnership service.

Transition to school

Pre-schools are now being asked to perform much like reception teachers with regard to planning the curriculum, planning for children with special needs and record-keeping. In theory, this should make liaison with schools easier. A uniform approach to record-keeping and the ability to produce useful information is a big step towards the recognition that pre-schools deserve. Now that early years settings are mentioned in the Code of Practice, recording for children with SEN has become more important. The recording pack in Appendix 1 will give a guide to the kind of records that pre-school settings and schools will find useful.

Pre-school staff should feel comfortable about setting up liaison procedures with the schools to which their children will move on. A discussion between the SENCOs about a child can make a lot of difference to the settling-in period. Pre-school staff should feel confident about passing on vital information. Confidentiality is often an issue, but most parents will be comfortable with the idea of SEN records being passed on to the school. It should be made clear that if schools know well in advance about children coming to them, they will be in a position to make the best possible provision for those children. Schools' SEN budgets are usually set in the spring term for the following autumn term, so the pre-school will need to make contact with a school well in advance.

Some schools and pre-schools have good liaison and transfer procedures. If you are concerned that you do not have a satisfactory transfer system, ask the school SENCO to visit or to meet you to discuss this. Some schools have set times for the children in the pre-school to make visits when they can see their classroom and meet their teacher, find out where the toilets are, where they will have their lunch, what the playground and toys are like, and where they will hang their coats – all the practical things which tend to worry children going to school.

For some children with more complex special needs, it may be advisable to make more visits and for their support worker to accompany them as appropriate.

Most children really look forward to going to 'big school' but there are some who find the prospect of leaving the familiar surroundings of their pre-school unsettling. If there are good systems in place for liaison and transfer it will ensure that the move for those children is as stress-free as possible. The more parents know about the procedures the better, as they will be reassured that their child is being introduced to the next stage in their education in the best possible way.

Tips for easy transition to school

- Make sure you have parental consent before forwarding SEN records.
- Set up informal and formal liaison procedures with all the schools you 'feed'.
- Get to know the school staff – especially the SENCO – so that the procedures above become more comfortable.

- Ask about making visits to school with the child/children.
- Keep brief records and information to pass on (IEPs etc., see Appendix 1).
- Tell the children well in advance about the move into school and discuss regularly in a positive way.
- Try to keep a professional distance – you can only be responsible for what the child does in your setting, so try not to worry about how he will cope when he leaves you. It is absolutely natural to think about how children will cope when they are in school, especially those you may have been supporting closely, but it is worth remembering that schools have well-established procedures in place to support children with SEN.

By following the steps outlined above, you can be confident that you have done all you can to 'smooth the way' for every child in your care to make the transition to school as happy as possible.

SECTION 5

Safeguarding

A good working relationship with parents and carers is essential for easing the transition of children into the nursery setting and maintaining a positive and collaborative approach to the child's welfare throughout their placement. Confidence in the well-being of their child while in the care of the nursery or pre-school will help to create a well-adjusted and relaxed child who will move on to the next phase of their education without too much anxiety. Parents and carers need to feel reassured that the setting is a safe and secure place for their children to spend their days, and the parents themselves need to feel listened to and feel that their concerns are treated with respect.

High-profile cases that have hit the headlines have increased public awareness of the vulnerability of young children, and the management of early years settings must make safeguarding, in all its meanings, a priority when arranging training programmes for all their staff. The implementation of a rigorously implemented safeguarding policy with an emphasis on accurate record-keeping and well-trained, vigilant personnel will help to reassure anxious parents that the setting they have chosen will have their child's welfare at heart. Providing parents and carers with a copy of the policy when they apply to have their child admitted to the pre-school, clear signage in the reception area informing parents and visitors of the name of the Designated Child Protection Co-ordinator for the establishment, and a clear display of literature on aspects of safeguarding (including subjects such as 'safety in the sun', advice helplines, healthy eating) will assist in reassuring parents that the setting is up-to-date and fully aware of current legislation and concerns.

Many early years settings use 'open' days not only to publicize their facilities to prospective new customers but also as a way of encouraging existing users of their facility to keep in touch and to take an active part in their child's education. Other settings have found that using parent 'workshop' sessions with a specific focus on a regular basis has been an effective way of reassuring parents and raising awareness of issues around early years education. 'Helping Your Child Start Nursery', 'Playing and Learning', 'Moving on to School' may be useful titles for such workshops, not only to help parents and carers to understand the role they and the setting jointly play in the development of their child, but also to promote the high priority that the setting places on safeguarding.

The management of the setting should ensure that their recruitment of suitable staff follows strict guidelines and that the setting applies a rigorous 'Safer Recruitment' policy. This must include, for instance, the checking of references, using a standard application form, and checking their accuracy. The days of personal recommendation and ad hoc appointments are long gone. Any gaps in employment history need to be investigated, and checking suitability through the Criminal Records Bureau/Independent Safeguarding Authority mechanisms must be carried out before anyone is allowed to begin work. Keeping all staff up to date with regular child protection/safeguarding courses provided by local authorities, safeguarding boards and the NSPCC will ensure, as far as possible, that everyone employed by the setting, including administrative staff and caretakers, is fully aware of their responsibilities.

Management obviously need to address their premises and equipment for 'health and safety'. The term 'health and safety' often produces groans and raised eyebrows, implying interference and over-the-top restrictions, but when young children who have not developed an awareness of their own risk are involved, it is vital that they are fully protected from harm in its widest sense. Premises obviously need to be clean, free from physical dangers, with adequate lighting, toilet facilities etc. But safe working practices and monitoring staff behaviour also need constant vigilance by all. The manner in which members of staff address one another and the children needs to be carefully observed, and instances of inappropriate comments should be swiftly addressed. Good role models will encourage good behaviour and positive relationships throughout the setting. A happy and secure staff team who feel confidence in their managers so that, if they report any concerns, they will be listened to and their issues followed up, will go a long way towards creating an emotionally stable and harmonious atmosphere. This in turn will reassure parents and carers that their child is in safe and caring hands.

It is a sad fact that some children do live in circumstances that are far from ideal. Families who move house frequently and do not appear to have a supportive network of family and friends may be particularly prone to living with stress, and may show indications that cause staff to be extra vigilant for signs that the children need extra support or safeguarding. If staff do observe behaviour or physical signs that cause concern, it is important that these are accurately recorded and processed in accordance with the safeguarding policy. The senior member of staff with the designated responsibility for safeguarding needs to ensure that all staff and any volunteers are fully aware of how child protection concerns must be managed. Confidentiality needs to be maintained but, at the same time, the safety of the child is paramount, and members of staff need to be aware of their responsibility to record and report any concerns in the correct way.

The early years setting may well be the first time that children have socialized outside the home, and it may also be the first time that the parent/carer has been able to meet with others outside the immediate family. It is therefore quite possible that a member of staff will be the first person who becomes aware of difficulties that the family are experiencing – financial, emotional or physical – and they need to be in a position to react appropriately and be able to signpost parents and carers towards the right sort of assistance. This is an important role as, of course, the pre-school setting has its own function to perform and prioritize. As well as making staff aware of policy and procedures and how to refer concerns through the right channels, the provision of literature, agencies' contact telephone numbers, and awareness-raising publications may prove useful. Displaying a small lending-library of self-help books covering a range of topics – from taming toddlers to cooking for allergies – might be a way of alerting parents and carers that the nursery is somewhere they can access information. The noticeboard of the nursery can be a discreet and useful place to display details of contact lines and help centres – those who are aware that they need to get some advice will be able to take down the relevant numbers directly into their mobile phone without being observed picking up specific literature. There is a wealth of publications around (including this series of *Tried and Tested!*) which would be appropriate for inclusion in the library, and early years settings that share premises with, for instance, schools or health centres will be in a good position to combine resources. Settings can also obtain free literature from a wide range of organizations and agencies, including the NSPCC, Childline, Healthy Schools, the NHS and the local Safeguarding Children Board as well as a wide range of commercial companies and supermarkets which nowadays produce useful publications on healthy nutrition, eyecare etc. It is quite likely that parents and carers themselves may have access to information that could usefully be made available to the setting.

As well as a copy of the Safeguarding policy, which should be provided to all employees when they take up employment (and staff should sign a form to say that they have read it), compulsory attendance on training courses on safeguarding and subsequent updates, the Staff Handbook should include specific direction on the use of mobile telephones and other electronic devices within the setting. All staff should be made aware of the restrictions on the use of cameras, camcorders and camera phones, and the setting's administration of first-aid guidelines, lone working, and transportation of children in staff cars policies must all be strictly adhered to.

When children reach the age for transition to the next phase of their education, the early years setting can do much to reduce the anxiety that this big step can cause. Those settings which share premises with the next phase in formal schooling are in a particularly good position to arrange informal visits to (and from) the school, but it is not uncommon for tensions to increase, and sometimes for unexpected or unwanted behaviours to arise. To many, references to 'big' school, school 'dinners', assemblies and detentions by other family members (particularly older siblings) can raise anxieties in both child and parent, and most early years settings will arrange for information sessions or visits to allay fears and give opportunities for parents and carers to ask questions and fact-find. Some parents will need reassurance that their child's behaviour may change as the time to move on becomes imminent. Children vary in their readiness for transition – some may be becoming a little bored with the pre-school and be keen to start something new, whilst others will be resisting the idea of change and will revert to more immature behaviour, maybe hoping that they will be allowed to stay put in the security of the pre-school. A visit to the new setting may do much to reduce anxiety for the child and the parent. Some parents may actually be more concerned than their offspring – a different or a longer, more complicated journey, or a new and perhaps apparently intimidating group of parents at the school gate, may cause real angst for some inexperienced parents. Inviting parents who have already experienced the transition process into the pre-school to meet with 'first timers' may be one way of preparing for a successful transfer away from the security blanket of the pre-school. Again, schools with attached nurseries often have well-established routines for engaging parents and carers, but parents who, for instance, have used employment-based or completely independent settings will probably need signposting to the often bewildering range of education available. The pre-school may need to remind staff that the families need to make informed choices, and staff should not, even inadvertently, direct parents towards (or away from) specific schools. Children differ in their personalities, and parents' own experiences will also have a bearing on which school will suit them. The early years setting needs to provide unbiased information and at the right time – families who leave it late to get a school place finalized may be disappointed or cause uncertainty-based anxiety in their child, who picks up on the chatter from their peers about their new school, uniform, new pencil cases and packed-lunchboxes and wonders what is in store for them.

Children who live in split households, possibly spending weekends and weekdays in different locations, may be particularly worried about transition to a new educational setting. If staff in the pre-school are aware that parents are having difficulty sorting out a mutually acceptable or convenient school, and particularly if they have noticed a change in the child's behaviour such as becoming quieter, reverting to more immature activities and behaviour or acting out in some way, it may be possible to set up a meeting to help sort matters out. Choice of school has to be the parents' decision, but impartial advice and informing parents of the effect that not knowing where they will be going every day after their time at pre-school ends is having on their child, may make a workable compromise easier to accept.

Cultural and social expectations may also have an influence on how a child deals with transition to the next phase, and staff will need to be alert to inaccurate perceptions around, for instance, strict discipline in Key Stage 1 or having 'loads' of homework. The conversations overheard from much older brothers and sisters sometimes get misconstrued, and the anxious four-year-old may pick up unrealistic expectations of lots of writing and having to carry about large bags of books. Inviting the class teachers from the local primary schools into the pre-school just to say 'hello' will at least go some way to paving the way for successful transition.

Case study

Danny has recently started at the pre-school and is brought in promptly each day by both his mother and father. He is a polite boy and the parents seem to be happy with the setting, and he leaves them quite happily. Once his parents leave the premises Danny initially plays contentedly with the activity to which he has been taken. However, when he is later given a choice of activity to play with, Danny becomes very confused, sometimes just curling up in a ball on a cushion in the book corner, and more recently he has begun rush around the setting without stopping, grabbing items from each area and dropping them anywhere. He rejects efforts of the staff to calm him down and settle to an activity. He eventually tires himself out and goes and lies down on the cushions. He leaves with his mother at the end of the session without difficulty but always appears subdued.

Staff were concerned that these outbursts occurred on a daily basis and there appeared to be no consoling him or distracting him. The Head of the pre-school asked Danny's mother to come into the setting at the end of the session to discuss his behaviour. His mother explained that they had moved house from another part of the country recently and were now living in an upstairs flat and

Danny's father did night work, so Danny was not allowed to play with anything other than the toy that he was allowed that day. Danny's father did not like mess around the house, and this included Danny's playthings; he had decided that Danny should be allowed one quiet toy a day to keep the noise down and the house tidy. Staff realized that their more relaxed attitude to children's need to play with a variety of toys and to talk, laugh and shout when appropriate was too much for Danny to handle in one go. He was not allowed choice at home or to make a noise indoors, and when presented with what appeared to be an unlimited selection of activities, he simply over-reacted. His mother also said that Danny's father did not like her to go out and about without him, so taking Danny to the park or to a children's gym had not been possible. He had only agreed to Danny attending the pre-school when workmates had said that school was compulsory and Danny would be reaching school age within the next few months. She was anxious to get home as Danny's father would in all likelihood question why she was late picking him up. She added that he was very generous with items for the house and Danny did have some expensive (but largely unused) toys and games. The Head agreed that in the short term they would handle Danny's difficulty with moving on to further activities by guiding him to a suitable toy, and an adult would remain nearby to forestall any outbursts. They would monitor his ability to pick and choose toys and activities for himself and ensure that he had the opportunity to experience a wide range of age-appropriate things to do. It was agreed that Danny's mother would call in again in a week's time a few minutes before the session ended to see how he was doing.

After Danny's mother had left, the Head and two other senior members of staff met to discuss the issues raised by Danny's mother. They were concerned that not only did Danny appear to lead a restricted lifestyle at home, it was clear that his mother was not accessing the wider networks of support that young mothers frequently create for themselves. She was new to the area, did not appear to have family close by, and appeared to need to account for her whereabouts. Staff had encountered similar situations to this in the past and felt that this was potentially a very sensitive situation and were keen not to expose Danny's mother to cross-examination about any meetings or discussions. The Head suggested that Danny's mother might benefit from meeting with another sympathetic parent in the pre-school whose child was due to start school soon and who could strike up at least a casual friendship, and that as there were several useful leaflets on a variety of domestic abuse situations available, they could make these available for Danny's mother to look at when she picked him up. The staff felt it was too soon to jump to conclusions that the family were in immediate need for a pro-active referral to, for instance, Women's Aid. However, from their experience, this family needed support, and particularly the mother needed to become more informed about what an acceptable level of independence should be. The Head agreed that careful monitoring of Danny's demeanour should be undertaken and that every opportunity should be given to the mother to raise any concerns. It was felt that any indication of a request for help from either parent or a disclosure of any kind from Danny should be responded to as a priority.

APPENDIX 1

Recording pack

SEN register

Observation sheet

Observation sheet example

IEP blank

IEP Rehanah

IEP William

IEP tracking sheet

Meeting with Parents/Carers

Special Educational Needs Register

Name of setting:		SENCO:		
Date:				

Child's name	DoB	Stage SA or SA+	Key worker	Date added to/ taken off register

Observation Sheet

NAME:	DoB:	DATE:

PRE-SCHOOL:

REASON FOR OBSERVATION:

TIME:	OBSERVATIONS: record the context of the behaviour (the activity going on, people present etc.), the possible trigger for the behaviour (what happened immediately before), the exact behaviour itself – just as it happened (what you saw, not what you think about it).

ACTION:

Observation Sheet

| NAME: Brendan | DoB: | DATE: |

PRE-SCHOOL:

REASON FOR OBSERVATION: Ricky's mum has complained that he has been getting upset about coming to nursery because he says that Brendan punches him.

TIME:	OBSERVATIONS: record the context of the behaviour (the activity going on, people present etc.), the possible trigger for the behaviour (what happened immediately before), the exact behaviour itself – just as it happened (what you saw, not what you think about it).
10.30	Outside playtime. Weather is fine, so children have large play equipment out. Ten children, two staff. Ricky has made straight for the yellow tractor and is enjoying scooting it down the slope. As he stops to turn back 'uphill', Brendan runs over to ask if he can have a go. Ricky says 'No, I'm on it.' Brendan looks around, sees staff occupied with other children and punches Ricky in the back. Ricky starts to cry, gets off the tractor. Mrs B comforts him but he won't say why he is crying. Brendan scoots off on the tractor.
ACTION:	I talked to Ricky and Brendan together and told them what I saw happen. I explained to Brendan that it was a very unkind thing to do to punch Ricky and something we don't allow in nursery and school. I got him to say 'sorry' to Ricky. Talked to them about 'sharing' – asked how they could share the tractor. All agreed that they would take turns – two goes each before swapping. All staff to keep an eye on the situation and praise both boys when they are seen to be sharing toys and taking turns. Tell Brendan's mum what happened. Review situation next week in staff meeting (date...).

Individual Education Plan

NAME: DoB: PRE-SCHOOL:

PLAN NO: ACTION/ACTION PLUS DATE:

AREA(S) FOR DEVELOPMENT:

TARGETS	STRATEGIES, RESOURCES, CONTRIBUTIONS
1	
2	
3	

TO BE ACHIEVED BY: REVIEW DATE:

SIGNATURES: SENCO: PARENTS/GUARDIANS:

REVIEW
1
2
3

FUTURE ACTION

SIGNATURES: SENCO: PARENTS/GUARDIANS:

Individual Education Plan

NAME: *Rehanah* **DoB:** **PRE-SCHOOL:** Holly Lane Kindergarten

PLAN NO: **ACTION/ACTION PLUS DATE:**

AREA(S) FOR DEVELOPMENT: *Listening and attention skills*

TARGETS	STRATEGIES, RESOURCES, CONTRIBUTIONS
1 Rehanah will be able to sit on her own carpet square for a short story once a week with some adult support	Rehanah's key worker will sit next to her with a copy of the book being read and will draw Rehanah's attention to the story and pictures – Rehanah could take her carpet square with her to any activity requiring listening
2 Rehanah will tell her key worker what the first activity on her personal timetable is every morning and put finished work into the right box with minimal adult support	The key worker will go over what the first activity is and prompt Rehanah about what the task is and how she will do it – when it is finished Rehanah will put it into her 'finished' box
3 Rehanah will be able to carry out simple instructions 3 out of 4 times	Adults will give Rehanah only one instruction at a time whenever they want her to do something – when she has done it, the next instruction will be given. The instruction should be made personal by using Rehanah's name

TO BE ACHIEVED BY: **REVIEW DATE:**

SIGNATURES: SENCO: PARENTS/GUARDIANS:

REVIEW	
1	
2	
3	

FUTURE ACTION

SIGNATURES: SENCO: PARENTS/GUARDIANS:

Individual Education Plan

NAME: *William*   **DoB:**   **PRE-SCHOOL:** Holly Lane Kindergarten

PLAN NO: **ACTION/ACTION PLUS DATE:**

AREA(S) FOR DEVELOPMENT: *Social skills, confidence*

TARGETS	STRATEGIES, RESOURCES, CONTRIBUTIONS
1 William will play a game with one other child and an adult for a short period every day	William's key worker will set this up and provide the language role model and appropriate encouragement
2 William will choose the book at story time twice per week when he is asked by his key worker	The key worker will explain to William that he is in charge of choosing the story and will give him a reminder beforehand so that he does not feel under pressure
3	

TO BE ACHIEVED BY: REVIEW DATE:

SIGNATURES: SENCO: PARENTS/GUARDIANS:

REVIEW
1
2
3

FUTURE ACTION

SIGNATURES: SENCO: PARENTS/GUARDIANS:

Individual Education Plan – Tracking Sheet

NAME:	DoB:	DATE:
KEY WORKER:		PRE-SCHOOL:

DATE:	TARGET: (1, 2 OR 3)	COMMENTS:	DATE ACHIEVED:

Meeting with Parents/Carers

Pre-school:	**Date:**
Name of child:	

Key worker:

Parent/carer:

Points discussed

Action

Signatures: Parent/carer: Key worker:

APPENDIX 2

Rehanah

Admission

On the admission form completed by the parents for Rehanah's entry into pre-school, there was nothing to indicate that there were any problems.

Rehanah started at the pre-school when she was three years and five months old: her mum would have liked her to start sooner but waited until Rehanah was fully toilet trained. She attended pre-school for three sessions each week. On entry into pre-school, staff noticed straight away that Rehanah was more active than most of the other children. This was particularly evident during the more structured times, for example during snack time and story time. She had difficulty concentrating and flitted from activity to activity, not really playing with anything in particular. She would often climb over other children to reach an object, interrupted adults when they were talking and often talked 'off topic'.

When adults gave instructions to the group as a whole, Rehanah sometimes did what was asked but often appeared to ignore them. She particularly enjoyed pushing a buggy around the hall and would play with this for much of the session, banging into other children and tables.

Staff discussion

Rehanah's key worker raised concerns about the child after only two sessions. She talked to the supervisor and SENCO and all agreed that Rehanah needed to be closely observed, but that she might just need an extended settling-in period. It could be that Rehanah had little or no experience of large groups.

Observation

It was decided to focus on observing Rehanah during story time and during the free play session. This was to gain an impression of how Rehanah behaved in two contrasting situations. Over a period of four weeks, information was gathered about what Rehanah was doing during the story session and what activities she was choosing during the free time session.

Staff meeting

The key worker and the SENCO met to discuss Rehanah's progress.

Observations indicated that Rehanah was disruptive during every single story session. She constantly shuffled about on her hands and knees, disturbing the children all around her, and she shouted out and interrupted the story. During the free play sessions, she invariably chose the buggy, ignoring all the other toys and not allowing other children to share.

Action from staff meeting

It was decided to focus on the behaviour at story time and also to discuss concerns with Mum.

Meeting with Mum

Key worker and SENCO spoke to Mum who was surprised to find that staff were concerned about Rehanah. The key worker explained that Rehanah had not taken note of what she had said on several occasions and asked Mum whether hearing had ever been investigated. It was suggested that Rehanah should be taken to see the GP, who could organize a hearing check. The key worker and SENCO discussed some strategies they could use to help Rehanah to sit with the other children during story time. They asked Mum if she would mind their contacting the area SENCO for some ideas. Mum agreed with this.

Discussion with area SENCO

The area SENCO came into the pre-school to discuss some managing strategies based on the information the pre-school gave her. (These strategies are outlined in Case Study 5.) The area SENCO suggested that they focus on one or two strategies over the next few weeks. She also advised that the staff should monitor what was working and did more of that. The area SENCO said she would contact the pre-school in about four weeks by phone for feedback.

Second meeting between staff and Mum

Prior to this meeting, Mum had informed the pre-school that Rehanah's hearing had been checked and found to be normal. The area SENCO had also contacted the pre-school to see how things were going. She was told that there had not been much progress. The area SENCO offered to help write a more structured programme if Mum agreed.

At this meeting, the feedback from the pre-school was that the strategy employed of sitting Rehanah close to an adult while listening in a small group, was not working well enough. Rehanah still poked other children and wandered off. They explained to Mum that an area SENCO could come in and help them to write an individual programme. They explained that this meant putting Rehanah's name on the Special Needs Register and working on some very small targets in a more intensive way.

At this meeting, Mum mentioned that the health visitor had had some concerns about Rehanah being 'constantly on the go'. Mum seemed happy with the involvement of the area SENCO.

Provision (implementation of the plan)

The pre-school SENCO, the key worker and the area SENCO discussed and worked out some targets to go on Rehanah's Individual Education Plan and a recording mechanism (see Appendix 1 for a tracking sheet). This plan was to be shared with all the staff working in the pre-school and closely adhered to.

(See Rehanah's Individual Education Plan on p. 108.)

The area SENCO advised the staff to review the plan after about half a term, or before then if the targets had been met.

Review of IEP meeting

The SENCO and the key worker found that working on smaller targets was having more of an impact on Rehanah's behaviour. Targets 1 and 2 were being met and Rehanah could sit on her own for 3 minutes before wandering off. Rehanah continued to have difficulty in carrying out simple instructions. This raised concerns about her understanding. The SENCO and the key worker decided that it could be a good idea to ask Mum if they could refer Rehanah to a speech and language therapist. They decided that they would need more help with Target 3 (carrying out simple instructions). When they received some advice they could write a more focused target. It was agreed that the key worker should feed back informally to Mum.

Meeting with Mum

The key worker had an informal meeting with Mum to discuss the above. She explained that the staff didn't know enough about speech and language areas and needed some advice in order to design a proper programme for Rehanah. Although Mum did not fully accept that Rehanah had problems in this area, she agreed to the pre-school staff contacting the speech and language department for advice.

Information from the speech and language therapist

The speech and language assessment picked up mild comprehension difficulties and gave the pre-school some ideas they could use in their programme. Included in the report was reference to the fact that Rehanah had proved difficult to assess as she constantly roamed around the room. The speech and language therapist suggested a further assessment to investigate attention difficulties.

Action in the pre-school

The pre-school continued to work on the Individual Education Plan, targeting listening and attention skills and reviewing them regularly. Rehanah was making better progress in listening and comprehension areas. She continued to have difficulties with attention to task and concentration. After about two terms, the pre-school recommended that Rehanah be assessed by a paediatrician. Mum was beginning to recognize that Rehanah was more difficult to manage at home. She was not listening to instructions and having temper tantrums when she couldn't have her own way.

Outcome

Mum decided to become involved in Rehanah's Individual Education Plan. She focused on helping her to develop better listening skills and gradually Rehanah began to follow simple instructions. Mum used appropriate rewards for wanted behaviours and tried not to give Rehanah attention for the temper tantrums. The paediatrician recognized that Rehanah had some difficulties regarding behaviour, especially concentration and attention, but was reluctant to make a formal diagnosis at this stage. She said she would see Rehanah at regular intervals.

The area SENCO who was supporting the pre-school advised that they should continue to work on small step targets to maintain progress.

Transfer into school

A copy of the Individual Education Plan with reviews was sent to school. A meeting was arranged concerning Rehanah's admission needs. The school recognized the support Rehanah had been given and were in a position to carry on meeting her needs at School Action level of intervention.

Social and emotional development checklist

It is important that any checklist is used with sensitivity. It should not be used to highlight what the child cannot do or to create unrealistic expectations. Instead, it should be seen as a very rough guide to the developmental steps most children take between the ages of two and five.

Age 2–3 years

- Increasing co-operation with parental requests: will *usually* do what is asked.

- May prefer to play alongside other children rather than with them.

- Finds difficulty in taking turns and sharing.

- Needs help to resolve problems with peers, e.g. if another child will not let him play with a toy.

- Carries out simple instructions, e.g. bringing or taking objects from room to room.

- Sits with adult to share books for five minutes.

- Says 'please' and 'thank you' when reminded.

- Makes attempts to help parent/carer with chores.

- Plays 'dressing up' in adult clothes.

- Makes a choice between, e.g. a cake or a biscuit, when asked.

- Shows understanding of feeling by verbalising, 'Maddy is hurt – she's crying.'

- Shows own feelings such as fear, affection etc.

- Beginning to respond to 'obvious' humour.

Age 3–4 years

- Sings and dances to music.

- Imitates other children regarding the following of rules.

- May become angry if things don't go his way, but beginning to control feelings – less chance of temper tantrums.

- Greets familiar adults without reminder.

- Follows rules in adult-led activity.

- Asks permission to use a toy being played with by another child.

- Increasingly says 'please' and 'thank you' without reminders.

- Is able to the answer the telephone and talk to a familiar person.

- Will take turns in a game or reaching into biscuit tin etc.

- Cooperates with adult requests 75% of the time.

- Stays in own garden/playground area.

- Plays near and talks with other children when engaged in own activity.

- Often prefers to play with others, wants to please friends.

- Likes to dress himself and increasingly tries to be independent.

Age 4–5 years

- Asks for help when having difficulty.

- Contributes to adult conversation.

- Repeats rhymes, songs or dances.

- Is able to work alone at an activity for up to 20 minutes.

- Will apologize without a reminder.

- Will take turns with an increasingly larger group of children (8 or 9).

- Will play cooperatively with other children, forming small groups that sometimes exclude others.

- Shows less physical aggression (hitting others), but uses verbal threats – 'I'll kick you, I'll tell my dad.'

- Beginning to understand the power of rejection – 'You can't be my friend.'

- May lie to avoid getting into trouble – 'It wasn't me!'

- Dresses and eats with minimum supervision.

- Engages in socially acceptable behaviour in public.

(Adapted from various sources for use with settings in Medway LEA.)

GLOSSARY

Autistic Spectrum Disorder (ASD) a developmental disorder that is characterized by social and communication difficulties

cognition how a child thinks and learns

emotional development the way a child controls and expresses his feelings

expressive language spoken language, talking

language delay limited and/or immature use of language

language disorder a difficulty with the understanding of words and their use

neurological associated with the brain and nervous system

receptive language understanding what is said

self-esteem the way we see ourselves – a child with high self-esteem has a positive picture of himself

social the way a child relates to his peers and adults and how he is able to respond to systems and organization

social awareness the ability to act in an appropriate way in different settings, e.g., organized groups such as pre-school settings

speech disorder this could be a difficulty with pronouncing single or combined sounds and/or sentence structure

structure giving structure to an activity or a day's activities means planning and organising things to good effect

FURTHER READING

Barrow, Giles, Emma Bradshaw and Trudie Newton (2001), *Improving Behaviour and Raising Self-Esteem in the Classroom*. London: David Fulton Publishers.

Bender, Pamela Stone (1997), *How to Keep Your Kids from Driving You Crazy: A Proven Programme for Improving Your Child's Behaviour and Regaining Control of Your Family*. Chichester: John Wiley & Sons.

Drifte, Collette (2001), *Special Needs in Early Years Settings: A Guide for Practitioners*. London: David Fulton Publishers.

Fabel, Adele and Elaine Mazlish (1999), *How to Talk so Kids will Listen and Listen so Kids will Talk*. London: Avon Books.

Glenn, Angela, Jacquie Cousins and Alicia Helps (2005), *Tried and Tested, Play and Learning in the Early Years*. London: David Fulton Publishers.

Green, Dr Christopher (1992), *Toddler Taming*. London: Vermillion.

Lear, R. (1996), *Play Helps*. Oxford: Heinemann Educational.

O'Brien, Tim (1998), *Promoting Positive Behaviour*. Essex County Council.

Phelan, Thomas (1995), *1–2–3 Magic: Effective Discipline for Children 2–12 Years*. Glen Ellyn, IL: Child Management Inc.

Roffey, Sue and Terry O'Reirdan (2001), *Young Children and Classroom Behaviour*. London: David Fulton Publishers.

USEFUL ADDRESSES

Down's Syndrome Association
155 Mitcham Road
London SW17 9PG
Tel: 020 8682 4001
Email: info@downs-syndrome.org.uk

National Autistic Society
393 City Road
London EC1V 1NG
Tel: 020 7833 2299
Email: nas@nas.org.uk

OASIS
Office for Advice, Assistance, Support and Information on Special Needs
Helpline: 09068 633201

Parentline Plus
Unit 520
Highgate Studios
53–57 Highgate Road
London NW5 1TL

Pre-school Learning Alliance
69 Kings Cross Road
London WC1X 9LL
Tel: 020 7833 0991

Picture Exchange Communication System
Pyramid Office
226 West Park Place
Newark DE 19711
USA
Tel: 001 888 732 7462
Email: pyramid@pecs.com

Social and Emotional Behaviour Difficulties Association
Church House
1 St Andrews View
Penrith
Cumbria CA11 7YF
Tel: 01768 210510

Sure Start Unit
Level 2
Caxton House
Tothill Street
London SW1H 9NA